Titles in the series

www.amazingstoriesbooks.com

LATE-BREAKING
AMAZING STORIES™

HURRICANE KATRINA

SURVIVAL STORIES

Courage in a time of tragedy and confusion

by Dee van Dyk

Altitude Publishing

PUBLISHED BY ALTITUDE PUBLISHING LTD.
1500 Railway Avenue, Canmore, Alberta T1W 1P6
www.amazingstoriesbooks.com
1-800-957-6888

Extreme care has been taken to ensure that the information contained
in this book is accurate and up to date at the time of printing. However,
neither the author nor the publisher is responsible for errors, omissions,
loss of income or anything else that may result from the information
contained in this book.

All web site URLs mentioned in this book were correct at the time of
printing. The publisher is not responsible for the content of external
web sites or changes which may have occurred since publication.

In order to make this book as universal as possible, all currency
is shown in US dollars.

Publisher	Stephen Hutchings
Associate Publisher	Kara Turner
Canadian Editor	Frances Purslow
U.S. Editor	Julian S. Martin
Charts	Scott Dutton

We acknowledge the financial support of the Government
of Canada through the Book Publishing Industry Development
Program (BPIDP) for our publishing activities.

ALTITUDE GREENTREE PROGRAM
Altitude Publishing will plant twice as many trees as were used
in the manufacturing of this product.

Cataloging in Publication Data
Van Dyk, Dee
    Hurricane Katrina survival stories / Dee van Dyk.

(Late breaking amazing stories)
ISBN 1-55265-320-X (American mass market edition)
ISBN 1-55439-522-4 (Canadian mass market edition)

1. Hurricane Katrina, 2005. 2. Disaster victims--United States--Gulf
Coast. 3. Rescue work--United States--Gulf Coast. I. Title. II. Series.

QC945.V35 2006	363.34'922'0976	C2005-907410-8 (Cdn)
QC945.V35 2006a	363.34'922'0976	C2005-907423-X (U.S.)

In Canada, Amazing Stories® is a registered trademark of Altitude Publishing
Canada Ltd. An application for the same trademark is pending in the U.S.

Printed and bound in Canada by Friesens
2 4 6 8 9 7 5 3 1

"My take was that there were plenty of people that were in charge, but nobody wanted to take charge."

Wayne Rogaczewski, Gretna, Louisiana resident

CONTENTS

National Hurricane Center Director Max Mayfield at
the Hurricane Center in Miami sitting in front of a
screen showing an infrared satellite image of Hurricane
Katrina on Sunday, August 28. For more on the
development of the storm, see pages 19–38.

Floodwaters from Hurricane Katrina cover a portion of New Orleans, a day after Katrina passed through the city.

This part of Slidell was flattened by Hurricane Katrina.

Local residents arrive at a ramp to the
Superdome after being rescued from
their homes, August 31, 2005.

Thousands of displaced people await buses
to depart the Superdome, September 2, 2005.
At one point, there were 20,000 people
sheltering in the Superdome.

People evacuated from areas flooded by Hurricane Katrina rest in a ticket area at the Louis Armstrong International Airport, September 3, 2005.
See pages 49–65 for more about the role of the airport as a shelter from the storm.

Members of the Oregon National Guard cruise through flooded streets September 5, 2005, in a light armored vehicle. Thousands of military personnel arrived in New Orleans to help with the relief and rebuilding effort.

A FEMA search and rescue worker pets a stray
dog in New Orleans. For more on the story
of pets that were left behind, see page 111.

Animal rescue expert Blair Mase wets down a Gulfport
Marine Oceanarium dolphin Eli on the transport boart
in Gulfport, Mississippi, September 20. For more on
the story of the Oceanarium, see page 99.

THE GULF STATES LOCATOR MAP

CHAPTER 1

Hurukan's Daughter

In the tropical waters off the coast of the Bahamas, Hurukan, the Mayan god of storms, stirs. From the heavens, thunderstorms crackle, while forked fingers of lightning reach for the brewing waves of the Atlantic. The waters are very warm here, easily reaching the 80 degree Fahrenheit (27° Celsius) temperature necessary for extreme weather. A slight rotational twist of a tropical wind, and Hurukan's daughter emerges, hungry.

Tuesday, August 23, 2005, 5 p.m.

The center of a tropical depression lumbers toward Florida at a cautious speed of eight miles (13 km) per hour, with winds gusting to 35 miles (56 km) per hour. This is noted by the National Hurricane Center. Tropical Depression Twelve is expected to strengthen to a tropical storm by Wednesday.

From Enid, Oklahoma, Aaron Wesson, meteorologist and extreme weather enthusiast, watches the new tropical depression take form. Father of four, with another on the way, Aaron monitors his public weather site at www. wxchat.com. It's early yet, too early to see the developing storm as anything more than lightning and winds spinning in cyclonic promise.

While Wesson monitors the weather offshore, life goes on in the city of New Orleans. Unaware of the trouble brewing in the Atlantic, residents and tourists go about their business as usual.

Canadian newlyweds Amanda and Gord Goulding are honeymooning in the Big Easy.

Their closest brush with hurricanes to date has been the drink of the same name, so popular in New Orleans's establishments. Made with rum, more rum, even more rum, and fruit juice, the hurricane drink is a favorite at the restaurant that created it: Pat O'Brien's.

Entergy businessman Wayne Rogaczewski is busy maintaining a business and family life, the former keeping him in St. Paul, Minnesota, and the latter bringing him home on weekends to New Orleans, Louisiana.

In the New Orleans Ninth Ward, Judy Carter, a retired schoolteacher, continues to recover from a stroke. Judy is no stranger to extreme weather, having survived Betsy, a strong Category 3 storm that hit New Orleans in 1965 and left 75 dead in her wake.

Hy McEnery, a New Orleans street minister and member of a Special Forces unit of the military, is a few short weeks away from deployment to Iraq. There's much to be done before he leaves.

And at Johnny White's—the New Orleans Bourbon Street bar that never closes—regulars and tourists alike gather to hoist a brew and enjoy the ambience of one of North America's most celebrated cities. Swinging in and out of the cut-out window of the famous strip club known as Big Daddy's, the curvaceous legs of a mannequin in fishnet stockings and pink high-heel shoes beckon passers-by. At Pat O'Brien's Courtyard Restaurant patrons sip hurricane drinks and munch on alligator tenderloin and crawfish nachos in front of the famous flaming fountain.

It's already been a banner season for hurricanes and, even as Tropical Depression Twelve builds toward storm status, her brother tropical storm, Jose, weakens as he moves over the mountains of central Mexico, having never attained hurricane strength.

Ninety-five miles (153 km) from the gathering storm, it has begun to rain in Nassau, Bahamas. Locals are accustomed to the storm

HURRICANE SEASON 2005 ,

The National Oceanic and Atmospheric Administration predicted an above-normal hurricane season for 2005. In fact, it would prove to be one of the busiest storm seasons on record. Katrina was named the most destructive storm to hit the United States.

Hurricane	Dates	Intensity	First Landfall	Deaths
Dennis	July 4–11	Category 4	Haiti (July 7)	5/U.S. 32/Cuba and Haiti
Emily	July 10–21	Category 4	Jamaica (July 16)	5/Carribean
Irene	August 4–18	Category 1	No landfall	
Katrina	August 23–30	Category 5	Florida (August 25)	1,300+/U.S.
Maria	September 1–10	Category 3	No landfall	
Nate	September 5–10	Category 1	No landfall	
Ophelia	September 6–17	Category 1	North Carolina	
Philippe	September 17–23	Category 1	No landfall	
Rita	September 17–24	Category 5	Gulf of Mexico	100+/U.S.
Stan	October 1–5	Category 1	Southwestern Gulf of Mexico (October 4)	672/Mexico
Vince	October 9–11	Category 1	Spain	
Wilma	October 15–25	Category 5	Yucatan Peninsula (October 22)	25/Mexico and U.S.
Beta	October 26–30	Category 3	Nicaragua	
Epsilon	November 29–	Category 1	No landfall	

season and its perils, having rebuilt after Hurricane Frances—a Category 4 storm of the 2004 hurricane season. In Columbus Tavern overlooking Nassau Harbour on Paradise Island, unconcerned tourists enjoy the catch of the day and down Bahamian coffee.

A tropical storm warning has been issued for Nassau, Cat Island, the Exhumas, Long Island, Rum Cay, San Salvador, the Abacos, Andros Island, the Berry Islands, Bimini, Eluethera and Grand Bahama Island. But this is paradise after all, and the threat of a looming storm seems distant. The locals simply hunker down for the four to eight inches (100 to 200 mm) of rain forecast for central and northwestern Bahamas. It's business as usual in hurricane alley.

It's business as usual for Aaron Wesson as well, as this Oklahoma-based meteorologist watches the storm develop. Aaron is fascinated by extreme weather and has developed a public weather site dedicated to bringing extreme weather discussion to weather experts and

HOW A HURRICANE FORMS

A hurricane needs three conditions to form: warm water (minimum 80°F (27°C), moist air, and converging equatorial winds.

Hurricanes usually begin as thunderstorms off the west coast of Africa, moving out over tropical waters. The warm storm air sucks moisture from the warm waters of the ocean surface. As it rises, an area of low pressure is created at the surface of the water.

The storm begins picking up speed, with air rising faster and faster, filling the low pressure area and sucking warm air off the ocean waters, while driving cooler air down.

The storm fuels itself with warm, moist air as it moves across the ocean, picking up speed and strength.

To be classified a hurricane, winds must exceed 74 mph (119 kph). As the winds build, the air pressure at the center of the storm drops, forming the elliptical eye of the storm. The eye is usually between 10 and 40 miles (16 to 64 km) wide and extends from the bottom of the storm to its top, chimney-like. In the eye, the air is calm and the sky is blue. But around the eye, Mother Nature has a temper tantrum in a most spectacular display of power. Torrential rain accompanies horrendous wind.

An average hurricane is 300 miles (483 km) wide and reaches 40,000 to 50,000 feet into the sky.

As the hurricane moves over warm oceanic water, it continues to gather strength. Only cooler waters or land will break its deadly spell.

amateurs around the world. It is frequented by extreme weather enthusiasts and fellow meteorologists. Together they sift through the weather/climate data, looking for clues that will lead them to the ultimate storm. On August 23, the available data led them to believe that the storm would hit Florida but was unlikely to threaten the Gulf.

The United States has seen more and more people settling and building along its coast. Beach property is prime real estate and, at least for part of the year, it offers idyllic conditions to its residents. Hurricane season runs from June 1 to November 30 and, since 1995, the Florida coastline has seen an increase in the number and intensity of tropical storms. Forecasters had predicted a banner year for hurricanes in 2005.

For some, this relentless increase in storm activity has resulted in hurricane fatigue. "People don't realize the amount of work that's involved in preparing for a hurricane," says Silvana Soleri, a travel writer based in Delray Beach,

Florida. "There are so many decisions to make, so many things to do, and everybody is after the same things. You go to the store to get non-perishables and the shelves are just about empty. Batteries are hard to find. Unless you've stockpiled these things in reserve, you can find yourself up the creek."

Silvana heard about Katrina's approach little more than a day before the storm made Florida landfall. "I hadn't heard anything because I didn't listen to the news. It can creep up on you and that's what happened with me with Katrina. A neighbor told me a hurricane was heading in our direction, but I didn't really believe her. I thought she probably misunderstood, because I figured I would've heard."

Her neighbor was right, as Silvana discovered when she checked the local weather station. With a sense of resignation, she kicked into hurricane mode.

"The last thing that I was going to do was bring the shutters down, so that at least I could have some daylight to do what I needed to," says Silvana. The shutter timeline is tight. Waiting too long makes it a wet, uncomfortable job. Pulling the shutters down too early means sitting in the gloom longer than necessary. By the time Silvana's shutters were in place, the rain had begun in earnest.

Silvana's preparations were done. "Around 6 o'clock in the evening it picked up hard. Our lights flickered for awhile, but they never went off completely for any length of time."

At this point, many still thought Hurricane Katrina would be a relatively minor hiccup

---

CONDITIONS OF A HURRICANE

1. **Location:** Hurricanes are tropical, forming in the ocean near the equator.
2. **Cyclonic Winds:** Hurricane winds cycle around a central eye, moving counterclockwise in the northern hemisphere and clockwise in the southern hemisphere.
3. **Wind Speed:** To be called a hurricane, a storm must have a minimum sustained wind speed of 74 mph (119 kph).
4. **Low Pressure:** A hurricane's eye will always be an area of low pressure. Extremely powerful hurricanes will have a very low barometric pressure.

on the 2005 storm season chart.

Thursday, August 25, 2005

Katrina strengthened to a Category 1 hurricane a few hours before making landfall at 5:30 p.m. She blew into southeast Florida be-

HURRICANE CATEGORIES

The Saffir-Simpson Scale measures hurricanes on a scale from 1 to 5, based on the hurricane's intensity. It is a predictor of the amount of damage and flooding the hurricane will cause. A chart showing the different categories is included in the Amazing Facts and Figures section (see page 164).

tween Hallandale Beach and North Miami Beach with wind gusts measuring more than 90 mph (145 kph).

Across the affected Florida area, more than 1.2 million people lost power and 11 deaths were reported as Katrina whipped the state for four hours. By 1 a.m., Katrina had fizzled back to a tropical storm. But the reprieve was fleeting: four hours later she regained hurricane strength.

Back in Enid, Aaron continued to monitor the storm's growth. When the hurricane headed for the Everglades, Aaron began to worry. The Everglades would provide the potent ingredients necessary to fuel Katrina. "There's bound to be trouble when a storm crosses the Everglades because it's so warm and muggy. All that power, all that energy; it was just waiting to be sucked up into this beautiful storm."

Aaron scanned the reports and readings off the National Hurricane Center website, comparing their findings with his own. "There was one model that mentioned something about New Orleans. At first I didn't believe it, because it was only one model and when you're a forecaster, you look for an agreement of models. You don't usually pay attention to the rogue model."

Friday, August 26, 2005

As the storm's feeder bands continued to hit the lower Florida Keys, Katrina was upgraded to a Category 2 hurricane, heading up the Gulf.

"Katrina starts making a path for the Florida panhandle," says Aaron. "It looks like she could develop into a pretty strong Cat 4 because the Gulf of Mexico was warmer than normal—about 86° F (30° C). That's pretty warm and very, very favorable for a tropical system to develop and move."

In the Slidell office of the National Hurricane Center, Chief Meteorologist Paul Trotter also watched the approaching storm with concern. Weather conditions had combined to create a looping effect that could potentially bring the hurricane up the Gulf Coast to rip through Louisiana. "You can't let your guard down. If you have a system in the Gulf, then you're fair game. And that's what it came down to," says Paul.

Hurricane hunter aircraft indicated maximum sustained winds near 100 mph (161 kph) and the National Hurricane Center warned of a potential Category 3 or 4 hurricane. In the warm waters of the Gulf of Mexico, Katrina rapidly gathered strength.

That same day, Governor Blanco of Louisiana declared a state of emergency calling Katrina

HURRICANE HUNTERS

While most people are flee-ing the hurricane, hurricane hunters head right into the storm. A WC-130 plane, complete with a six-person crew, drops a weather-sensing canister attached to a small parachute into the hurricane. The canister transmits data (temperature, humidity, pressure, and wind speed) back to the plane. The onboard crew processes the information and then relays the results to the National Hurricane Center.

an imminent threat and warned of severe storms and high winds.

Saturday, August 27, 2005

As expected, the next morning the National Hurricane Center is-sued an advisory up-grading Katrina to a Category 3 hurricane, with New Orleans con-firmed in her sights. President Bush declared a state of emergency in Louisiana and authorized the Federal Emer-gency Management Agency (FEMA) to initiate aid. Ray Nagin, mayor of New Orleans, issued a voluntary evacuation order at 5 p.m. Saturday, saying the Superdome would open as a shelter of last resort for evacuees with special needs.

"This is not a test. This is the real deal," Nagin said. He encouraged New Orleanians planning to evacuate to the Superdome to prepare as for a camping trip. In response to the voluntary evacuation, highways out of the city began to fill with traffic and several major interstates were converted to one-way arteries out of the city.

Sunday, August 28, 2005

By early Sunday morning, Katrina had rocketed to a Category 5 hurricane with a minimum central pressure of 902 millibars, the fourth lowest on record for an Atlantic storm. Louisiana and Mississippi hadn't seen a stronger storm since Hurricane Camille in 1969.

In Slidell, meteorologist Paul Trotter continues to monitor the hurricane's approach. "We have had a lot of storms in the past that have followed that particular path. We've had Camille and Betsy. This storm (Katrina) was stronger than Camille, Betsy, Andrew, and Ivan put together. Its girth is what made it so disastrous. It wasn't a local storm like the others."

Further compounding Katrina's damage potential was her eye. "Katrina had an eye diameter of 40 miles (64 km) and, once the storm itself came toward the Louisiana coast, the eye started to explode and expand the wind field around it," explains Trotter. In contrast, Charley, a devastating hurricane in 2004, had an eye diameter of only 10 miles (16 km).

Sunday, August 28, 2005

At 11 a.m., for the first time in New Orleans history, the mayor issued a mandatory evacuation order. Ten "refuges of last resort," including the Superdome, were opened to accommodate the anticipated need for shelter from the storm.

The National Hurricane Center advised a storm surge of up to 28 feet (8.5 m) and issued a dire warning: MOST OF THE AREA WILL BE UNINHABITABLE FOR WEEKS PERHAPS LONGER ... AT LEAST ONE-HALF OF WELL-CONSTRUCTED HOMES WILL HAVE ROOF AND WALL FAILURE. ALL GABLED ROOFS WILL FAIL, LEAVING THOSE HOMES SEVERELY DAMAGED OR DE-

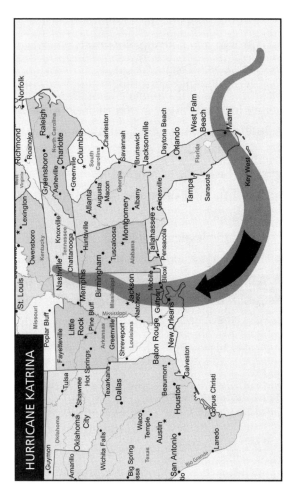

Hurricane Katrina grew in the Gulf of Mexico before landing in Louisiana.

STROYED ... POWER OUTAGES WILL LAST FOR WEEKS ... WATER SHORTAGES WILL MAKE HUMAN SUFFERING INCREDIBLE BY MODERN STANDARDS.

Amid fears about the hurricane, another concern loomed large. Much of New Orleans was built below sea level, with flood conditions controlled by a system of pumps and levees. In the event of levee failure, and in the absence of natural drainage, what would happen to New Orleans?

Would the levees hold?

Dr. Max Mayfield, Director of the National Hurricane Center, did not think so. "We were briefing them [the politicians] way before landfall ... it's not like this was a surprise. We noted in the advisories that the levee could be topped."

Meanwhile, Aaron

STORM SURGE

Storm surge is often a greater threat to human life and property than the high winds typically associated with a hurricane. Surge refers to the large wall of water—between 50 to 100 miles (80 to 161 km) wide—that crashes onto land when the hurricane makes landfall.

Wesson watched the hurricane's advance in amazement. "She was a Cat 5 on the 28th of August at 8 a.m. and her winds were 160 mph (257 kph) ... basically, New Orleans was in for it. Bad things were coming."

Monday, August 29, 2005

Katrina was downgraded to a Category 4 hurricane, still with devastating potential. She made landfall in Louisiana between Grand Isle and the mouth of the Mississippi River three hours later.

For the next few hours, the country watched as Louisiana was driven to her knees by the storm. The magnitude of the disaster was reflected in a statement made by Mayor Nagin early Monday morning. "I've gotten reports this morning that there is already water coming over some of the levee systems. In the Lower Ninth Ward, we've had one of our pumping stations stop operating."

In the Superdome, 10,000 evacuees watched as Katrina's winds ripped two holes in the Superdome's roof. Airports throughout the states of Louisiana and Mississippi were closed to air traffic, while terrified, stranded passengers waited out the storm.

A little more than 12 hours later, Katrina—the monster storm that shocked the country—subsided to a tropical storm. In the short space of a week, Hurricane Katrina morphed from swirling winds and warm temperatures to one of the most catastrophic hurricanes in American history. Only the unnamed hurricanes of 1900 and 1928 claimed more lives than Katrina.

CHAPTER 2

The Big Easy

Residents and visitors agree that there is nothing ordinary about New Orleans. Or New Orleanians. Outside of New Orleans, the mere mention of the fact that one is native to the city is enough to spark an enthusiastic discussion.

"When you tell people you're from New Orleans, they say, 'You're from New Orleans? I love that city,'" says Joseph Martin Bagnerise, his eyes sparkling mischievously. Born and raised in New Orleans, Bagnerise now makes his home in Calgary, Canada. When he talks about his old home town, his voice lights up with enthusiasm.

New Orleans has personality—a raucous energy that pulses from the city like a Zydeco beat. It's this personality that pulls 10 million tourists annually into the city, seduced by the city's well-deserved rep for memorable food and party-till-you-drop fun. But it's the undercurrents of her personality that native Orleanians know so well. In the minds of many, the ingredients making New Orleans unique ultimately influenced the many arms of the Katrina tragedy: evacuation, impact, rescue, and rebuilding. To understand Katrina's effect on New Orleans, one needs to understand New Orleans.

Nicknamed the "Birthplace of Jazz," New Orleans is home to such legendary musicians as Fats Domino, Harry Connick Jr., Jelly Roll Morton, Louis Armstrong, and Mahalia Jackson.

Food is a confluence of cuisine and culture here. Natives are careful to point out that it's Creole, not Cajun, that defines the flavor of the city. Visitors note only that some of the finest food in the country can be found in the city's 3,088 restaurants.

The same ethnic influences that make New Orleans cuisine distinctive make the city one of the most interesting architectural landscapes in the country. Residential architecture varies from district to district, often defining the history and culture of each particular area. Creole cottages and townhouses, American townhouses, raised center-hall cottages and villas, double gallery houses, and shotgun houses all contribute to the local historical architectural landscape.

The 78 square blocks named the French Quarter are famous for authentic Spanish, Colonial, and antebellum buildings. In comparison, the Ninth Ward is lined with shotgun houses—a style of home unique to New Orleans, but believed to originate in Haiti and Africa. A shotgun house is a narrow strip of rooms where, local legend

NEW ORLEANS ARCHITECTURE

Creole Cottage (c. 1790–1850)
Found in the French Quarter, these cottages are single story, ground level stucco or wood exterior homes set close to the property line.

American Townhouse (c. 1820–1850)
Found in the Central Business District or Lower Garden District, these narrow three-story structures are made of brick and stucco and feature an asymmetrical arrangement of façade openings.

Creole Townhouse (c. 1788–mid-1800s)
Predominately found in the French Quarter and surrounding neighborhoods, these two- to four-story structures feature iron balconies on the second and sometimes third levels.

Raised Center-Hall Cottage or Villa (c. 1803–1870)
Found in the Garden District, Uptown, and Carrollton, these one-and-a-half-story houses are raised two to eight feet above ground on brick piers.

Shotgun House (c. 1850–1910)
Found throughout New Orleans, these one-story linear houses sometimes have a second story set at the back of the house, called a camelback.

has it, if you shot a gun through the front door, the bullet would cut through every room in the house and exit the back door.

History affects every aspect of life in New Orleans.

Founded on the bend of the Mississippi River, New Orleans was claimed for Louis XIV in 1699, making it the only U.S. city in which French was the prevailing language for more than 100 years. The area was slow to settle, but a trade route by water was established, with crops of indigo, rice, and tobacco all produced on Louisiana plantations.

The French and Indian War left Spain in control of Louisiana at a time when Acadians were fleeing to the New Orleans area, having been driven from Nova Scotia, Canada, by the British.

Eventually the conquering Spaniards were absorbed into the predominantly French culture of the area and Louisiana was returned to France in 1800, eventually becoming the 18th state in

1812. Waterway access to the area from both the Gulf and the Mississippi River has always been important to the growth and development of the area.

In the mid-1800s, slave labor fed the plantations of the area and by 1850 New Orleans had become the largest slave-trading center in the southern United States. Racial struggles persist to this day.

Waterways continue to be vital to the economic health of the area, not only for commercial transport, but also as a feeder route for tourism and cruise ships.

Much of this city's personality translates into tourism dollars, but there's a darker side to New Orleans. Although murder statistics have dropped in the last decade, New Orleans' homicide rate is 10 times the national average.

But it's the geography of the city that would figure most prominently as Hurricane Katrina blasted through New Orleans. Shaped like a crescent cradling the Mississippi River, New

Orleans is surrounded by water: Lake Pontchartrain, the Gulf of Mexico, and the Mississippi River. The city itself is 5 to 10 feet (1.5 to 3 m) below sea level, depending on which part of the city you're in. Effectively, New Orleans is a bowl, surrounded by water.

It's no surprise that New Orleans is prone to flooding and the city protects itself with a series of levees and dikes. Rainwater is continually pumped out of the city. Above-ground crypts replace underground burial sites in local cemeteries.

On Monday, August 29, 2005, all aspects of the city—its culture, demographic population, geography, and history—converged as the lid slipped off the jambalaya pot that is New Orleans.

Since moving to Louisiana in 1982, Wayne Rogaczewski has learned to appreciate all of these aspects of this vibrant city. He has also come to respect hurricanes and their destructive potential. However, he wasn't initially worried when he first heard of Katrina's existence. "I was watching the football game on the television in my corporate apartment in St. Paul, Minnesota," says Wayne. "It was the night before the storm was due to make landfall in south Florida and the commentators mentioned that the hurricane was in the area. I checked the weather channel, which showed the forecasted path of Katrina." The path appeared to miss New Orleans.

The next day—Friday—Wayne flew home to New Orleans, as usual, to spend the weekend with his wife, Sherrie, and their 16-year-old son, Brett. They watched the weather channel together that night, as Katrina gained strength. Then they prepared for possible evacuation.

"We boarded up the house and put the patio and lawn furniture into the garage," recalls Wayne. "We live off a golf course and I always hear the birds. We have a lot of tree frogs and ducks." Ominously, Wayne noticed the normal chatter of the resident wildlife was gone. The golf course was silent.

Wayne called the airports, only to find that airlines were canceling flights beginning Sunday. Still not overly worried, Wayne decided to change his flight time to Saturday to ensure getting back to St. Paul in time for work. As a further precaution, Sherrie and Brett decided to fly to South Carolina on Saturday to stay with family.

Wayne scrambled to pull things together; worried that possible water damage might affect his computer and work files. He told Brett to pack enough clothes for three days. He didn't think they would need to be away longer than that. He was mistaken.

Normally it takes Wayne 20 to 25 minutes to drive to the airport, but on this particular Saturday it took two hours and 20 minutes to maneuver through the thickening traffic.

From the safety of his apartment in St. Paul on Sunday, he watched the mandatory evacuation on television. "Putting people in the Superdome has happened other times; it's not all that unusual. Normally it's the shelter of last resort. It's usually used for the elderly and people with medical problems, but this time they opened it up to other residents of the city and started bussing in those people who didn't have transportation out."

On Monday morning, Wayne awoke and turned on the television for an update on the hurricane damage. "I'd been watching all the coverage and they were talking about the people still being at the Superdome and showing the damage to all the hotels. Basically, it looked like the city had dodged the bullet on this one.

"Then I heard that the levees had been breached and the city was filling up with water. I thought, 'That's not good.'"

CHAPTER 3

For Better or For Worse

Along St. Peter Street, Pat O'Brien's claims to serve more alcohol than any bar in the world. Its most famous creation is the "Hurricane," a mix of rum and fruit juice. Legend has it that when booze was scarce during World War II, bar owners stocked up. When Pat O'Brien's found itself with a 50-case surplus of rum, bartenders decided to use it up in a special drink poured into 26-ounce (769 mL) glasses shaped like hurricane lamps. That's the story as locals tell it.

Few cities in North America rival the New Orleans *joie de vivre*. The French Quarter is the throbbing heartbeat of this city, seducing visitors with the promise of non-stop fun.

"Bourbon Street is a party street," says visitor Amanda Goulding. "The drinks are insane; they're about 150 proof. Fifteen dollars will buy you two huge drinks that will set you on your ass."

For newlyweds Gord and Amanda Goulding, a honeymoon in New Orleans was the highlight of their wedding plans. Living in St. Stephen, New Brunswick, they felt that New Orleans was far enough away to be exotic, close enough to be affordable. It was to be the holiday of a lifetime.

The Gouldings landed in New Orleans on the afternoon of Sunday, August 21, anxious to see the sights.

The night they arrived, they had dinner at the Quarter Scene Restaurant (QSR), a popular

Bourbon Street eating establishment known for its Pain Perdu (New Orleans French toast with grilled bananas), Pecan Catfish, and a host of po-boys named for the characters in *A Streetcar Named Desire*. (Tennessee Williams dined regularly at QSR.)

Seduced by the romantic magic of the city, the newlyweds spent the following days in a blur of tourist activity. With so much to see and do, they didn't hear about Hurricane Katrina's approach until Saturday, August 27—little more than a day before her Louisiana landfall.

"We heard about the hurricane on Saturday," says Amanda. Scheduled to leave the next day, the newlyweds were beginning to wind down their honeymoon. "We were in our hotel room watching television. Until then, we hadn't called our parents, but when we heard about the hurricane I wanted to call and tell them we might leave early."

Amanda's parents were out, but Gord's mom, Ella, answered. Hearing the worry in her daughter-in-law's voice, Ella attempted to steady her. "You're going to get out before the hurricane; you're going to leave before it hits," she said.

Although Ella's words calmed the newly-weds, they now counted the hours until their honeymoon would be over and they could return to the safety of home.

News of possible evacuation made them realize how serious their situation was. "I began to cry. I told Gord that I didn't want to be here," recalls Amanda.

The couple calmed themselves by making contingency plans. They decided to leave early Sunday morning. That way they would be at the airport in case an opportunity arose to fly out early.

Unknown to Gord and Amanda, the Louis Armstrong International Airport activated its Emergency Operations Center (EOC) at 11 a.m. Saturday, August 27. The airport's essential personnel were put on alert. They were instructed to secure their homes and report to work. While the couple was still in their hotel room planning their escape, their airline had already made the decision to cancel their flight out.

With growing anxiety, the Gouldings continued to watch the hurricane coverage from their hotel room. Early Sunday morning, they decided not to wait for their pre-paid airport shuttle; they called a 6 a.m. cab to take them to the airport.

It took the Goulding's cab two hours rather than the usual 25 minutes to get to the Louis Armstrong New Orleans International Airport in Kenner. Traffic was snarled with people evacuating the city. Upon arrival, the newlyweds were relieved to see their flight time unchanged on the departure screens of the airport. Unable to check their bags until 10 a.m. for their 2 p.m. flight, the couple ducked into the Acme Oyster Bar—the only airport food venue still open—for breakfast. They marveled at their timely escape.

But when they returned to check the departure screens at 10 a.m., the Gouldings were horrified to discover their New York flight connection had been canceled. Panicked, they approached an American Airlines representative who told them they would be placed on a flight to Atlanta, which would at least get them safely out of the hurricane's projected path.

"The airline rep came back about 15 minutes later and told us there were two seats on AirTran to Atlanta." Relieved, the Gouldings shelled out the extra money for the Atlanta detour.

As the departure screens showed more and more canceled flights, the Gouldings decided to hedge their bets by gathering some supplies. Amanda set out for water.

Standing in an airport kiosk line, Amanda heard the clerk explain that water bottles would be rationed. Amanda bought peanuts, three bottles of water, and three breakfast bars.

When she returned, Gord gave her the bad news: they were stuck in New Orleans with Hurricane Katrina quickly approaching. It was time to notify their families.

Amanda tried to call her parents—Heather and Daren Langlais—but she couldn't reach them. Then she called Gord's mother. Ella could hear the panic in her daughter-in-law's voice again and knew she had to calm her down. "You can't think rationally and escape a hurricane if you're panicked," she told Amanda. Once more, Ella's words calmed Amanda.

Amanda returned to Gord to formulate a plan. "Gord and I had both quit smoking, but that day we bought a pack of cigarettes. That was the only thing that kept me rational."

With some spare change, the Gouldings got a luggage cart and packed their bags onto it. It was noon by then, and they knew for sure that they would not be making a miraculous escape from the approaching hurricane.

There was nothing to do, except wait and pass the time talking to fellow stranded passengers. Some had been through hurricanes before and did not mince words with the newlyweds. "It's bad," they said. "It's not going to be pretty."

Gord and Amanda crowded around an airport television reporting on the advancing storm. "They kept saying that if you don't get out of the city you might die," recalls Amanda. "That was the scary part—the leading up to the hurricane—because nobody knew anything. No one was saying anything except 'get out of the city.' But we couldn't get out of the city."

Gord tried to calm his terrified wife. "It's okay," he told her. "We'll get through this."

With Katrina's winds approaching land at 175 miles (282 km) per hour, many airlines decided to cease service to New Orleans earlier than expected. The last scheduled passenger flight that departed Louis Armstrong New Orleans International Airport that day was a Continental Airlines plane at 4:30 p.m.

The airport officially closed two hours later, with 150 to 200 passengers and 40 to 60 airline employees and their families left to wait out the storm. Their numbers swelled by 60 more when nearby New Orleans residents also evacuated to the airport. Airport staff and facilities were stretched to the breaking point.

Night approached and stranded passengers and residents moved into the main ticket lobby, away from windows, skylights, and glass doors. The tension was palpable as people waited for the approaching storm.

Gord and Amanda made camp in a small nook by a ticket checkout. With a few chairs and the luggage cart, Gord walled off a shelter and laid some airport mats down on the floor to soften their living space.

An impromptu community, borne of shared fear, sprang up around them. People protectively watched over each other's belongings and looked out for each other.

"We met a wonderful couple, Linda and Ed, from Florida," remembers Amanda. "They had been through hurricanes and they told us it was going to be scary, but that we would be all right."

Secretly, Amanda feared there were be a tidal wave or a flood that would roll over the airport. Would she and Gord die on their hon-eymoon? Her fear was compounded as she lis-tened to a battery-operated radio belonging to a fellow passenger. "We heard all the horrible stuff that was going to come," Amanda says. "I got sick to my stomach. In the washroom, a lady beside me gave me some antacid."

Afraid the power would fail while she was in the washroom, Amanda hurried back to their makeshift shelter. The antacid had calmed her stomach and, despite a bad back, she was so tired from the crying and tension that she was able to nap briefly.

"Gord could sleep through anything," Amanda says. And he did.

Monday morning, August 29, 2005

As the storm approached, ferocious winds tore at the building and torrential rains pounded its exte-rior. Weakened, the building roof sustained leaks, and at 3 a.m. fire alarms sounded. The water and extremely high humidity had shorted them.

"The lights looked like disco lights flashing," Amanda remembers. "We were ready for the power to go. But then there was this shaking and the wind whistled like a train."

Commercial power to the airport failed at 5:20 a.m., shutting down the air conditioners and activating the back-up generators. It was about to get hotter and much more uncomfortable.

Katrina's full fury was unleashed on the airport at about 8 a.m. People moved to the center of the main terminal to escape the increasing problem of roof leakage in Concourse C. Parts of the airport—including the canopy over the departures ramp—sustained more damage, and the airfield from North Kenner began flooding.

"Part of the ceiling caved in on the other side of the airport," says Amanda. "The roar of the hurricane winds was deafening." The Gouldings wondered if their last hours on earth would be spent in the airport. "But we were so blessed, we got nothing compared to what everyone else got. We were in the bad part of the storm for about three hours. The most stressful part was waiting for the water to hit, but it never did.

"We weren't allowed near the glass windows, so we couldn't see outside. We just waited. There were a lot of kids running around. People, blankets, mats, and chairs were everywhere."

By noon Katrina had passed, but the problems and difficulties remained. "There was a sense of loss in the building," says Amanda. Having survived Katrina, the Gouldings were painfully aware of the losses of those native New Orleanians around them. "A lot of people who were in there knew they'd lost everything. But they were less concerned about that than they were about their families."

In the wake of the storm, the air was hot and oppressive. Inside the airport or outside, there was no escaping the overwhelming heat. Having survived the hurricane, the Gouldings now waited along with everyone else—for rescue. They were hot, sticky, and dirty.

However, the rescue initially planned by the airport was suspended when helicopters began arriving. They transported evacuees from the rooftops, hospitals, and roads of New Orleans. Air conditioning units were set up in a makeshift triage area on the upper level. The Airport Rescue and Fire Fighters (ARFF) turned their attention to the new evacuees, many of whom had injuries requiring treatment. Among the stranded airport passengers were 31 doctors and nurses willing to pitch in and help.

Now the airport began to see casualties, not from its own population, but from the new arrivals, many of whom were old or sick. The air was thick with sounds of pain and the stench of urine and feces. In an evacuating helicopter on the airport tarmac, a woman gave birth to a healthy baby—a ray of sunshine as a counterpoint to the dark circumstances in the wake of Katrina.

But not all the news of incoming evacuees was so hopeful.

"We had people die and ladies have miscarriages," recalls Michelle Duffourc, Public Relations Manager for the airport. "The volunteer doctors stopped the labor of one woman so we could evacuate her before she delivered. We had no means of sustaining the baby or caring for the mother if she had a troubled labor or delivery."

Meanwhile, Amanda and Gord were running low on water and the snacks they'd purchased before the storm. CA One Services, an airport foodservice operation, cranked out simple meals three times a day with a limited staff of two or three, plus family members. Their resources were stretched further as more New Orleanians flocked to the airport looking for shelter.

With 95° F (35° C) temperature, backed up toilets, and unanswered questions, the morale among the trapped passengers was flagging.

"For all we knew we could be there for a month," says Amanda. "I called my parents every day, but sometimes the phones would act up. On the radio we heard about people getting raped in the Superdome, although I never felt threatened by anyone in the airport. Everyone was good, but I worried they would ship us to the Superdome."

Tuesday morning, August 30, 2005

Reed Barnes, the airport's Training and Flight Information Display Systems Manager, approached Gord and asked if he'd help clear debris from the runways. Gord jumped at the opportunity to join a group of working volunteers.

The north-south runway of the Louis Armstrong New Orleans International Airport opened for day operations at 2 p.m., and the first flight taxied onto the runway at 3:55 that afternoon.

With something to do and an end in sight, the spirits of those in the airport began to lift.

The Gouldings split a chocolate voodoo doll they found packed in their luggage and discussed their options.

"By then, we were in a good mood, talking and playing knuckle wars and thumb wars to pass the time," recalls Amanda. They debated whether or not to leave the airport in search of supplies, but decided they didn't want to risk missing a bus or flight. The rumor in the airport was that it might still be a long wait—as long as a couple of weeks—before they would be able to leave New Orleans.

Tuesday, August 30, 2005

Finally, after days of waiting and wondering, the Goulding's honeymoon adventure was over. They boarded a flight to Dallas, Texas, where they spent the night before catching a flight to Bangor, New Brunswick.

At the Bangor airport, their families waited for the newlyweds, holding up homemade signs: Welcome Home, Mandy and Gord; Congratulations, You Survived Hurricane Katrina!

"I wanted to kiss the ground," says Amanda. Their marriage had survived the worst, now it was time to celebrate.

CHAPTER 4

Xavier University

Judy Carter lives in the 5400 block of Burgundy Street in the Ninth Ward of New Orleans. The Ninth Ward, bordered by Lake Pontchartrain on the north and the industrial canal to the west, has a reputation as a tough neighborhood. Jazz heavy-hitter Fats Domino is from the Ninth Ward.

Judy has experienced more than one hurricane in her 60 years, but Katrina was an experience like none before. Part of a trend toward in-creasingly powerful hurricanes, Katrina came at the midpoint of the most active hurricane season on record. Katrina would be the first of a trifecta of hurricanes (including Rita and Wilma) that would set the record for the most Category 5 hurricanes in a season. This season would also produce the highest number of landfalls of major hurricanes (4) for the United States, the highest number of named storms (25), the most hurricanes (14), and the lowest pressure (882 millibars, set by Wilma). The 2005 season would also become the most costly hurricane season on record, shattering the 2004 record of $45 billion in damages.

For many in the Ninth Ward of New Orleans, this would be the catastrophe of their lifetime. And it would cost many their lives.

Judy's warm, rich voice hints at laughter and, even as she tells her story of loss and terror, she's quick to find humor in the incidentals of her adventure. Judy has lived in the same house on Burgundy Street for 38 years and, as is fairly

common in New Orleans, her daughter, Courtney, lives in a house on the same property.

Friday, August 26, 2005

Courtney worked security at Harrah's casino in
New Orleans, but Friday found her home on a
regularly scheduled day off. Judy and Courtney
tuned into the television to watch the storm—
their habit when storms threatened the Gulf. Judy says, "We al-
ways watch the storms because you never know what's going to happen. You have to be prepared for what might be coming."

HARRAH'S

Harrah's employed more than 6,000 people at its affected Gulf Coast properties prior to Hurricane Katrina. Sixty-eight percent of the employees who worked at Harrah's New Orleans lived in the Ninth Ward.

As it became obvious the storm was going
to be bad, and that it might have New Orleans in
its sights, the mother and daughter put together
a few bags, with an eye to possible evacuation.

"We packed clothing and insurance policies. And we packed some Vienna sausages," she pauses for a throaty chuckle at her Vienna sausages confession. "We didn't know where we might have to go or for how long."

Along with the rest of Louisiana, the two women spent a stressful Saturday tracking the storm's approach.

Sunday, August 28, 2005

When Mayor Nagin announced the mandatory evacuation, the Carters were prepared for it. Judy and Courtney don't have a car, so relatives had made plans for them. At about 2 o'clock Sunday afternoon, Judy took one last look around the yard and stopped to talk to a neighbor. Judy's block on Burgundy Street is populated by long-time residents. An informal block watch keeps residents aware of strangers and unsavory types who might be passing through the area. "I told Freddie where we were going to go. That's one very good thing about our neighborhood: we all kept track of each other."

Judy's cousin, Rawn Davis, is the Physical Plant Manager at Xavier University. He picked up the women early Sunday evening and drove them to the university. In all, 350 students plus 60 staff and their families joined Judy and Courtney at the university.

"One of the ladies who was there had a portable television and I had a radio, and we were just listening and looking out of the window," recalls Judy. "We were out of harm's way on the third floor of the administration building, along with staff and their family members. The students were in dorms in a separate building."

The first casualty of the storm was the

XAVIER UNIVERSITY

Xavier University is an historically Black Catholic university, ranking first in the nation in placing African American students in medical schools (Association of American Medical Colleges ranking). Xavier claims to have graduated 25 percent of practicing African American pharmacists. Just over half of Xavier's students are from the state of Louisiana. Founded by the Sisters of the Blessed Sacrament in 1925, Xavier reported Hurricane Katrina damages in excess of $90 million.

husband of a former Xavier University employee, Eloise Simmons. "She [Eloise] and a couple of her family members were with us, one of which was her husband. He died. He just died," says Judy. Only much later would they discover Simmons had died of heart failure—one of many indirect casualties who succumbed to the stresses of the storm.

As Sunday wore on, Katrina's imminent arrival was underlined by the weather around them. The rain pounded the earth and began to fill the canal by the university.

"When we had arrived, there was no water in the canal. But by about 6 o'clock in the evening when I was walking about, oh my heavens, it was half full."

Judy and Courtney and their fellow evacuees settled in to await the storm. "We just walked around and watched and listened to the news. That's all we did. Even when night fell, we were all up listening, talking, and waiting for the storm. In the morning, Katrina hit. Oh, it was terrible, terrible rain. The rain was very, very hard. It lasted about four hours."

Courtney, a self-described water person, felt calmed at first by the rains. For her, the sound of rain mitigated the terrible fury of Katrina's winds. Later, she would find the relentless rain disturbing.

In 1965, Judy and her family survived Hurricane Betsy. "I know what it sounds like—the wind, the howling. But this storm was bigger. [It generated] a lot of noise. Once the wind and the rain came, we just got in a corner and stayed still. There was nothing to do but wait."

Despite the driving winds and rain, Judy and her fellow evacuees continued to feel relatively safe. Xavier University, founded in 1925, was sturdy and sound. "Mother Katharine Drexel—she's a saint now—founded Xavier high school and the university. She was watching us," Judy maintains.

When the storm had finally passed, the evacuees ventured out to survey the damage.

"The water came in the building to the fifth step of the first floor. Someone had parked his van right in front of the building and the water came up so high, we couldn't see his van. It had disappeared."

The danger of the storm now apparently past, the group's primary concern shifted to the mother of one of the security guards. She had had her last dialysis treatment on Friday before the hurricane. "We were really concerned about her. We didn't want another person to die," says Judy.

In the immediate post-hurricane days, life ran relatively smoothly for the Xavier evacuees. Food was ferried by boat to the dormitories and to the administration building from the nearby convent of the Sisters of the Blessed Sacrament. There was enough drinking water, and floodwater was used to flush toilets manually.

While they continued to eke out a survival for themselves, nobody wanted to think about what had been left behind.

As the floodwaters continued to rise, the university administration developed an evacuation plan. They arranged for boats to transport the Xavier students and faculty to safety. Meanwhile, eight buses from the Grambling State University campus struck out for New Orleans, and they were joined by three additional buses provided by Senator Cleo Fields.

Thursday, September 1, 2005

Judy relives the rescue with gratitude. "My daughter came to me and said, 'Mama, just take one bag. We're going downstairs because they've come to get us. They're rescuing us.'"

"I'm only 4'11" and as I stood looking at the boat, I wondered how I was going to get into it. My daughter said, 'Mama, they're going to get you in there and I'm going to help you.'" The crippling from Judy's stroke impeded the transfer slightly, but she made it.

Judy and her daughter, along with three others, were taken to the Interstate-10 Expressway to wait for the buses from Grambling. After dropping them off, the boat turned around to pick up more evacuees. The boat would make many trips before the day was over. "When all the people from Xavier were finally on the interstate, then other people started arriving. They weren't there before, but as soon as we were out there, other people started coming out to where we were. They must have been from the surrounding area."

The evacuees waited for nine hours on the hot interstate asphalt, the stifling, humid air wilting their hopes. Around them, the devastation of the storm and the flooding brought home the magnitude of their losses. "About the eighth hour, I started to be afraid the buses weren't going to come for us," says Judy. Others grumbled more loudly. "Some people were getting hungry. The lady who needed dialysis was with us, she and her husband. After about three hours, a helicopter landed near us. We told the pilot this lady was ill. They took the lady and her husband to a hospital."

The helicopters returned with food. "Now I know what the soldiers eat," says Judy. "It was like beef stew. We also had bread and even a piece of cake. It was good. We were very grateful."

Unknown to the evacuees, their buses had been delayed by post-hurricane road and weather conditions, so trucks arrived to take the weary travelers to the next point.

"The trucks were very high and people had to boost me up to get on the truck. Then they drove those trucks to another portion of the interstate right next to the *Times Picayune* [newspaper], where we waited for another three hours. After we got off the trucks, they had more people to look for and rescue."

As the spirits of the evacuees began to bottom out again, they saw police cars approaching. "The people in the police cars got out," says Judy. "Well, lo and behold, it was Jesse Jackson and Senator Cleo Fields.

"It was beautiful, because that was somebody giving us hope. Somebody actually wanted to see us survive. The parents were tired now, but the kids were really happy. It was a wonderful experience and one I'll never forget."

At 10 p.m., more than 12 hours after leaving the sanctuary of Xavier University, the evacuees were thrilled by the arrival of their buses, escorted by armed Louisiana State Police and National Guard units. "These army guys came from Crowley, Louisiana," explains Judy. "They had been scheduled to go to Iraq, but instead they were sent to New Orleans to get us."

The soldiers urgently told the group to hurry onto the buses. Other people had gathered—some angry and armed—and there was fear that shooting would break out and the buses would be hijacked. The evacuees ducked down low in their seats, in case of gunfire.

Luckily, they escaped without further incident.

Friday, September 2, 2005

The caravan of buses traveled through the night, arriving at the campus of the Southern University in Baton Rouge in the wee hours of Friday morning. Some of the exhausted travelers chose to stay in Baton Rouge. The rest, about 200 strong, traveled for another 4.5 hours to Grambling State University.

"When we arrived at about 6 or 6:30 a.m., people were greeting us, welcoming us. They had covered the gym floor with mattresses, made them up, and had soap and toiletries for us. One side was for students and the other for families. It was wonderful—towels, soap, and a shower," Judy laughs in appreciation, even though she has lost most of her worldly possessions.

"We stayed at Grambling for two days. Any student from New Orleans that wanted to go to Grambling State University was accepted right then and there."

Judy and Courtney's relief at being rescued was tempered with the news of how badly their city, and especially their Ninth Ward neighbor-hood, had been affected. An uncle, who had opted to stay behind, has never been located. A hole axed into the roof of his home suggests that he lived through the hurricane, but may have drowned in the levee breach.

Their own home, they discovered later from those who ventured back to look at the neighborhood, was completely demolished. Built around 1900, the shotgun house that contained their valuables and memories was gone. Constructed of sturdy bargeboard, it had withstood all that came before Katrina. But it crumpled under the one-two punch of Katrina and the levee breach. A few short weeks later, Rita would barrel through the area and further ravage the Ninth Ward.

Some argued that the Ninth Ward was completely unsalvageable. Others hinted that the choice not to rebuild the Ninth Ward would be tainted with a racial motive.

"Although the Ninth Ward—and New

Orleans—was a cultural gumbo pot, the majority of the Ninth Ward was African American. I'm making a guess, but maybe people thought that the African American community was the downfall of the city because of the crime rate and other factors. Then if you get rid of the Lower Ninth Ward, you get a different New Orleans," says Courtney Carter. She adds significantly, "But you can't have New Orleans without the African American community. It won't be the same. That huge melting pot that is New Orleans? It just got tipped over," adds Courtney.

For the Carters, the decision to leave New Orleans, at least in the short term, was easy. Judy's son, Mark Tillman, lives in Michigan and, with the help of his Alpha Phi Alpha fraternity brothers, put together enough frequent flyer miles to bring Judy and Courtney to stay with him.

Courtney sums up their losses. "We can't go back. We can't. Our area was hit twice; it was the hardest hit. The area we lived in is uninhabitable. Everything is water-logged. Infested. Contaminated. So the idea of going back to clean something up of that magnitude, well, there's nothing to go back to.

"People say you've got to move on and grow from this, but how do you? I can't believe this is happening to me. In the blink of an eye, everything is gone—memories, pictures, everything. It's all gone."

CHAPTER 5

Hell No, We Won't Go!

I n every hurricane, there are people who opt to stay put and ride it out. In August of 2005, approximately 20 percent of New Orleanians made that decision for a variety of reasons. Some were sick and unable to leave, some were unable to find transportation out of the city, and some were unwilling to leave their pets behind. Some felt they could safely ride out the storm.

Henry "Hy" Alfred McEnery III, an ordained southern Baptist street minister of inner-city youths and self-described survivalist, was one of the latter. A native of New Orleans, Hy can trace his ancestry back to some of the original settlers of the city.

Hy and his wife, Elizabeth (Libba), run the Laurel Street Bed and Breakfast, an Eastlake Victorian cottage built in 1891. Their home/bed-and-breakfast is a sturdy building of heart pine and cypress, both extremely strong and durable woods.

"I didn't consider evacuating because I live on the highest part of the city; this area will never flood unless you have a flood of biblical proportions," says Hy with a chuckle.

When he first heard about the approach of Hurricane Katrina—several days before it actually hit New Orleans—Hy was busy tying up loose ends in preparation for a seven-month deployment to Iraq, as a sergeant in the National Guard.

"We didn't know the hurricane was going to come into New Orleans, but we knew it was out there and we knew it could be a bad one," says Hy. "But we've seen many of them in the past and they didn't necessarily hit. In fact, we had one that was coming to us back in the late '90s and it was going to be really bad. It was called Georges and right before it hit us, it turned to the side. I did a radio show at the time, and I put together a prayer for New Orleanians to say. They read the prayer every hour as the storm barreled down on us. Right at the last moment it veered off to the east and we were delivered from that blow.

"We get threatened every year and you kind of get the jitters. You get apprehensive. You think, 'I've got enough pressures and issues I'm trying to work out. The last thing I need in the middle of all this is a hurricane.' In fact, at that point I had two weeks to get ready to go overseas. My unit was being activated for military duty in Iraq. Plus I have this ministry that we run and it keeps us extremely busy."

But Mother Nature waits for no man and by Friday afternoon, August 26, Hy—along with the rest of New Orleans—began to realize that the potential for Katrina to rip up the Gulf of Mexico and into New Orleans was very real.

While Hy felt comfortable about his own ability to ride out the storm, he was not so sure about those under the care of his street ministry. He had a year's supply of food in his house and an unlimited water supply from a cistern system holding water from downspouts. He had also filled up all his bathtubs, and a 55-gallon drum with water. "I do a lot of backpacking, a lot of camping. I'm in a special forces unit with training to survive in very difficult situations," says Hy. "With all my training and all my past experiences from the time I was a kid, I was very comfortable to be here through it."

But Hy knew that the youngsters in his street ministry wouldn't think to put water in bottles. "They wouldn't have the money to buy water and they wouldn't think to fill empty bottles from the tap. A lot of them were in the areas that flood really badly and they just wouldn't be prepared for it. It wasn't a place for them."

Hy, a devout Christian, believes that a friend of his had a vision about Katrina. In response, a small group of churches in New Orleans had begun to prepare two years earlier. "He had a vision from God to prepare New Orleans for a very destructive hurricane that God told him was going to come. He told everybody that two years ago, and we've been hearing about the Big One for a long time, so I really feel that he was listening to the Lord. When I say that God told him, I don't mean he had a vision or an apparition or that an angel came and told him. He just got this real strong sense that God was speaking to him and telling him to get ready. He's a doctor and he does a lot of inner-city mission work with the poor. So he organized an evacuation plan. When Katrina hit, he got buses and vans and cars that the members of the little churches owned and they got a bunch of people out." Hy pauses, his voice tired. "I tried to get my kids out, but I couldn't get them all out. In many cases, their parents would not leave. I don't even know why."

Ultimately, about 50 of Hy's charges (including their families) stayed behind. On Saturday, Hy began to prepare his house for the approaching hurricane. His wife, Libba, and stepdaughter, Elizabeth, evacuated to Little Rock, Arkansas, while Hy stayed behind to focus on the task at hand.

Sunday, August 28, 2005

As gale force winds hit the city, two of the families from Hy's street ministry called. They were anxious to evacuate to Baton Rouge. He told them it was too late; they were going to have to hunker down and wait it out. He advised them to fill all available bottles with water, to gather food, whatever they would need for survival.

"People don't always think of simple things like toilet paper. I told them how to put together a bug-out bag: you put all the most important things in one bag, so if you've got to leave in a hurry you can at least grab that and run." Hy's own bug-out bag was ready. Just in case.

As he waited, Hy kept the weather channel on, hoping and praying that Katrina would be diverted from New Orleans at the last possible moment. He was fully aware of the storm's potential to damage the city.

HY McENERY'S BUG-OUT BAG

- change of clothes
- some basic toiletry articles—toothbrush, toothpaste, razor, deodorant, toilet paper
- towel
- food
- water
- flashlight
- batteries
- radio
- good book to read, your Bible
- some writing paper and a pen
- knife or some simple tools, eating utensils

Monday, August 29, 2005

Finally, at about 3 a.m., an exhausted Hy went to bed to try to sleep. He awoke three hours later from the force of the storm. Around him, the storm raged, winds tearing at his home and destructive rains seeking entry. Although the windows were shuttered, he peeked out as best he could. Dawn was breaking in the city, as he anxiously went from room to room, checking for leaks and ready to move things around as necessary. Confident that his own home would survive the prying fingers of Katrina's winds, he worried about the families in his ministry who had stayed behind. Would their homes survive? Would they survive?

Outside, the storm howled, sucking the breath in and out of houses, causing them to buckle and collapse. Trees snapped and metal tore, becoming deadly projectiles in Katrina's swirling winds.

Hy maintained his vigil until about 4 p.m., when he sensed the storm beginning to weaken. It was time to venture out to see what kind of havoc Katrina had wrought.

"Sides of houses had collapsed and were exposing the whole inside of the house," says Hy. "Trees were down all over the place."

Driving was next to impossible because the city was littered with nails from the roofs, so at first Hy explored the neighborhood damage on foot.

He walked through the eerily empty streets to check on the nearby families of his street ministry. Although Hy would later discover that not all his charges had survived the evacuation, he was initially relieved to find those who had remained behind had survived. He began to coach them on preparing for the wait for rescue. "I kind of gave them the Dutch uncle talk. I told them, 'If you don't prepare yourself right now for what's coming, you stand a chance of making yourself very sick or even maybe dying.'"

Once Hy was sure his families were okay, he continued to explore his neighborhood, stopping to help out where he could. On his return home, he noticed more people had ventured out onto their front porches. One neighbor who had evacuated to a downtown hotel was back with a battery-operated television. He and Hy were shocked as they watched the post-storm scenes on the screen. "It looked like bombs had gone off, almost like the Oklahoma City bombing. A lot of roofs had blown off," says Hy.

The phones were still in service—although sometimes with poor reception—so Hy was able to call Libba and tell her he was all right. Although the electricity was out and Hy had a generator, he chose not to use it, opting instead to treat the first days of the aftermath as a camping expedition. He had survived the first day post-Katrina.

Tuesday, August 30, 2005

Hy awoke Tuesday morning to screaming and hooting outside. "It sounded almost like it was a celebration or something. I looked out the window and saw a couple of people who lived down the block. Their cars were jam-packed full of stuff."

The looting had begun.

Venturing out of the neighborhood, Hy encountered some policemen who were watching the looting; they told him martial law had been declared.

Under martial law, people are authorized to confiscate and appropriate whatever they need for survival, but Hy was disturbed to see people vandalizing. A mob mentality had begun to set in, he feared, and he worried about what they might be capable of.

Hy wondered what was happening in the rest of the city. He went onto the interstate, which offered a good vantage point to see what was going on.

What he saw disturbed him even more. "There were thousands of people, as far as I could see, walking towards the Superdome." What Hy didn't realize yet was that the levee breaches had begun. Phase Two of Katrina's destructive onslaught was the devastating floods that would send thousands of New Orleanians to the already troubled Superdome.

Hy drove down the interstate, where he spotted a group of people carrying a woman stretched out on a ladder. He pulled over and loaded the woman, along with a handful of older people and children from the group, into his van, promising to return for the others.

He would drop them off at the Superdome. "When I got to the Dome I saw five feet of water on the street. The streets were flooding," Hy recalls.

Around the Superdome and separated from it by a moat of water, clusters of people waited. Having evacuated to what they thought was safe haven, they found there was no food, no water, no restroom facilities, no medical aid, no shelter, and no access.

"I was expecting there to be National Guard troops all over the place. You know, the cavalry would come over the hill and save the day and everything would be okay. But it wasn't like that at all." As Hy watched, he saw a small convoy of large military trucks and a water buffalo [a large water tank] swinging around the bottom of the Superdome. "They can travel in five feet of water; they have snorkels and they're high above the ground. So I figured they were going to swing around and bring food and water to the hungry, thirsty people."

Relieved, Hy left his little contingent of evacuees and returned to pick up the ones he'd left behind. When he returned to the Superdome with them, the situation was worse. "I come back and there were no trucks. There was no water. The people were more desperate than when I saw them before."

Hy's best guess is that the military vehicles brought food and water to the Superdome, but left without loading up the stranded people outside and bringing them into the building.

He didn't have time to wonder about this, however, because the crowd began to gather menacingly around his vehicle. To the crowd, Hy's ministry van looked like it might be a government vehicle. They began to demand help and whatever he had. "I told them I was a local minister and I didn't have anything they were asking for."

He gave them a half-gallon of water, which was all he had in the vehicle. Then he decided it was time to head back home. The city had initiated a post-storm curfew and it was getting dark. "I could see the violence mounting. It wasn't smart to be out on the streets at night."

From that point on, Hy carried a gun, as did most people in the city. New Orleans had taken on the disturbing personality of a post-apocalyptic world. Gunshots echoed through the streets of the city.

With a lifetime of public service behind him, Hy's instinct was to look for a solution to the devastation he was witnessing. "Finally I realized that I could hit one of the stores, get some food and water, and bring it to the people in distress. So that's what I did.

"On Thursday morning, a fellow I had never met before showed up. He came from the Dallas Bible Church. His name was James Caffin and he came like an angel," says Hy, his voice filling with emotion. "He arrived with a big van full of food and water and all kinds of good stuff. He began to go out with me and help me."

The Quentin Road Bible Baptist Church of Lake Zurich, Illinois, also sent a team of four people and a truck loaded with food, water, and medical supplies to Hy. The Quentin Road team worked alongside him for four days, doing search-and-rescue work.

"We found one lady on Thursday. Her husband had died the night before and she would not leave." In dire need of medical attention herself, Violet Jackson refused to leave her husband until Hy performed a brief funeral ceremony for him. Ten days later, the National Guard would arrive to take Alcede Jackson's blanket-covered body from the porch bench of his Laurel Street shotgun house. Above Jackson's body was the homemade poster board tombstone fashioned by Hy. It read:

ALCEDE JACKSON

B - D Aug. 31, 2005 Rest in Peace

In the Loving Arms of Jesus

"For God so loved the world that he gave his only begotten son (Jesus) that whosoever believeth in Him, shall not perish but have everlasting life!"
– John 3:16.

Hy estimates it was close to 10 days after the hurricane before the organized effort of the government had any kind of impact. "When the cavalry finally came over the hill, the battle was over and it had mainly been fought and won by volunteers."

CHAPTER 6

The Animals of Katrina

Human beings are not the only creatures affected by extreme weather phenomena. Usually human suffering receives all of the press coverage, even though other forms of life feel the effects of such a catastrophic change in the environment. Hurricane Katrina was an anomaly. The story of some of the animals in the path of her destruction did reach the ears of television viewers and newspaper readers. One such story features the Marine Life Oceanarium located in Gulfport, Mississippi.

In the days prior to Katrina's Louisiana landfall, Mobashir "Moby" Solangi, owner and director of the Marine Life Oceanarium, watched Katrina cut a destructive path. He and his colleagues hoped she would not travel up the Gulf Coast to Gulfport. But as Katrina gathered strength and veered west, the staff of the Oceanarium came to terms with the very real possibility that they might feel the sharp side of her wrath. They scrambled to prepare the aquarium—home to 14 dolphins, 27 sea lions, and 25 exotic birds—for the rapidly approaching storm.

"In the past when we've had situations like this, the animals that were in low-lying tanks were removed from the park," Moby says. "In this case, we took six dolphins and eight sea lions."

The dolphins were transported to hotel pools—three each to a Holiday Inn and to Gulfport's Best Western—to wait out the storm. The eight sea lions, who didn't require a tank to survive, went to the curator's home to wait out the storm. The remaining dolphins and sea lions were left in a huge tank that has survived every hurricane from Camille to Katrina.

Gulfport reeled under Katrina's attack. Bordering Louisiana on the east side, this coastal community was hit more savagely than expected when the hurricane looped up the coast. Throughout Mississippi, 800,000 people lost power, 90 percent of coastline buildings were destroyed, and, along the Biloxi-Gulfport coast, casino barges were washed ashore. The immense storm surge pulled fish out of the ocean and spit them onto the beaches, their eyeballs burst from the pressure changes. Mississippi Governor Haley Barbour compared the devastation to that of the atomic bomb dropped on Hiroshima during World War II.

Although the tank containing the dolphins and sea lions did, in fact, survive Katrina, the tidal wave that came in was higher than the 30-foot (9.1-m) tank. The wall of water plucked the dolphins and sea lions from the park and flooded them into the surrounding area. The Oceanarium was destroyed beyond recognition. "As soon as we found out that our aquarium was swamped," says Moby, "we made arrangements for the six dolphins in hotel pools to be sent to the folks at Florida's Gulfarium in Fort Walton Beach for a more extended stay."

The sea lions displaced by the storm surge began resurfacing in strange places. "The sea lions started showing up two or three days after the hurricane, in different towns and different places. Each one was found under different circumstances," remembers Moby.

"We found them everywhere," echoes Emma Jarvis, a trainer from Oceanarium who participated in the rescue effort, "in people's back yards, under trucks, on people's front porch, in parking lots of what used to be hotels. We found one of our sea lions at the Oasis—a hotel with a lazy river [an elliptical pool]."

Although finding the animals was not

terribly difficult, storing and transporting them to a safe destination proved to be a more challenging task. "One of the sea lions turned up at an ice warehouse," says Emma. "The warehouse had a large garage door that was lifted all the way up and couldn't be closed. We found TC [one of the sea lions] there and we basically made a large barricade so he would stay there. All you need most of the time with sea lions is the visual of a barricade. If they have no reason to leave where they are, they won't. That's what we were counting on. We made a barricade around the opening of the warehouse."

With a large pickup truck and a spare animal crate, Emma and her fellow rescuers rounded up the other sea lions and transported them to the warehouse. "At that point, Gulfarium (Fort Walton Beach, Florida), SeaWorld (Orlando, Florida), and Gulf World (Panama City Beach, Florida) brought in trucks and crates to transport the sea lions from the warehouse to SeaWorld and Gulfarium."

SeaWorld Orlando is no stranger to potentially devastating hurricanes.

"Last year we had three big hurricanes come through Orlando," says Randy Runnells, one of two Assistant Curators of Mammals in SeaWorld, Orlando. He describes the process of preparing for a storm: "We have to make sure the animals are well fed before the storm hits. As soon as the main storm goes through, we make sure that all debris that blows into pools is cleaned up. We have a "ride out" crew that stays in our park, and hunkers down in one of our buildings during the hurricane. They're the first response to whatever needs to be cleaned out or if we have an emergency with our animals. They clean out the area around to make sure that none of the animals ingest anything. If the power goes out here at SeaWorld, we have back-up systems to run the pumps and filters to keep the water clean."

When Randy heard what was heading toward the Gulf Coast, he knew that SeaWorld might be called in to help. "In a crisis, it's wonderful that all these institutions work with each other. In a way we're competitors, but we're not. SeaWorld is a lot bigger than the other facilities, but when things like this happen, we all pull together. We made space for these animals. We're all here for the animals."

What followed is an incredible rescue story.

"Ron Hardy from Gulfworld, in Panama City, called to say that Oceanarium was in distress and needed a holding place for some of their animals," says Randy. "We mounted a crew and rented a truck and did a transfer, driving almost 1,000 miles within 24 hours to pick them up and bring them back."

The team consisted of Randy and three other members, all of whom are animal care specialists. Originally, the team planned to meet their sea lions at Gulfworld in Panama City Beach, but when they called en route, they discovered they would have to drive 60 miles (97 km) farther south—to Fort Walton Beach—to pick up the sea lions.

In Fort Walton, a transfer of eight sea lions in individual cages was made. One team member rode in the back of the truck with the animals, keeping them wet and monitoring their health and vital signs.

The first truckload of sea lions rolled into SeaWorld Orlando at about 8 p.m. They were unloaded and a second team of two traveled back to pick up the remaining six sea lions.

"I think the sea lions were a little stressed because of what they went through," says Randy. "They did, however, begin to eat within a day or two, which is a good sign. They had individual pools in their facility, but we didn't have an opportunity to do that. We had to throw them all together, but they all got along. As it stands right now, they're all doing pretty well."

While the sea lions were being rescued in relatively short order, the Oceanarium dolphins were not to be found.

"They had been swept away," says Moby Solangi. With no sign of the missing dolphins, the Oceanarium staff concentrated on rescuing and evacuating the sea lions. "Thirteen days later, when things had begun to calm down, we were able to secure a helicopter and we went out searching for the dolphins. We had one of our trainers in a boat." The Oceanarium crew would use the helicopter to spot the dolphins and then send the boat to check them out.

The dolphins were spotted almost immediately and the team onboard the helicopter radioed the boat. The trainers, following the helicopter's coordinates, brought whistles and a bucket of fish to the dolphin sighting.

Miraculously, in what Moby describes as the strangest phenomena he has ever seen, all eight dolphins had stayed together for the two weeks, waiting to be rescued. That they had remained together and all survived the ordeal surpassed Moby's hopes. "There were six females and two young males, and there were two mother-calf relationships in that group. Three of these animals were born in captivity. They would have no idea of the wild and wouldn't know what their prey was or who their predators were. Some of the other adults had been in captivity for 30 years or more, and they would have lost all instincts or knowledge of the area."

The dolphins were in very deep water and the rescuers were faced with the dilemma of how to catch them and how to bring them in.

The immediacy of their problem was lessened when they realized that the dolphins would come to the boat to feed. The rescue team lashed together two inflated rubber mats as a makeshift beaching platform for the dolphins. Eight feet long and four feet wide, the mats were then used in feeding the dolphins, who became accustomed to sliding up on the mats for their food, three times a day.

The next priority was to determine the condition of the dolphins. They were clearly not in good shape, since they had all lost weight. While at the Oceanarium, the dolphins had been trained to present and allow for blood to be taken. Moby and his team now relied on that learned behavior to get blood from the mammals to assess their health.

Blood tests revealed that the dolphins were dehydrated, a natural extension of their poor nutrition. Unable to tell what constituted food in the wild, some of the dolphins had ingested harmful matter. A few days into the rescue one dolphin vomited the head of a hammer, another regurgitated a pair of men's underwear.

"We pulled a big stingray spine out of one of the baby dolphins. They're curious. Apparently he saw something in the water and went to it. It was a stingray," says Moby. The team extracted a two-inch (5 cm) barb from the head of the dolphin.

While Moby and his team developed a rescue/transit plan, the focus was to keep the dolphins coming back to the makeshift beaching platform.

The dolphins stayed near the beaching platform for the duration of their rescue. "That was apparently their security blanket or security platform. If only they could speak, they could probably tell a good story," says Moby.

Their social structure was examined in an effort to see who was more dominant and who needed more help. The first to be beached and lifted out were those dolphins who were most compromised. It was important to keep the dominant ones behind until the last. In this way, the dominant dolphins kept the herd together until all were safely rescued.

The rescued dolphins were warehoused in a local hotel swimming pool until Navy temporary pools arrived.

Moby reflects on the whole experience with wonder. "Normally in the wild, male dolphins encountering females would try to corral them and get them into their herd. That didn't happen. Apparently some of the females were strong enough to ward off the intrusion from potential predators.

"These animals stayed together, which is

extremely unusual. Even though they were lost, they managed to maneuver their way to the shoreline and stick around the harbor."

In Moby's opinion, one driving force kept the dolphins together. "I think they all stayed together because they were all scared of the same things. Each one became the support of the others. That's being anthropomorphic, but there is no other explanation."

CHAPTER 7

Toonces's Wild Ride

Meanwhile, people's pets were also traumatized by the effects of Hurricane Katrina. People who evacuated to nearby shelters were barred from bringing pets and, for some, the inability to take a pet resulted in a decision to not evacuate.

"The day before Katrina moved ashore, as the devastating effects were being predicted and the animal welfare response was being crafted, the need for a single centralized data system became evident," says Betsy Saul, President and co-founder of the public charity, Petfinder.com. Within days, Petfinder.com—an on-line searchable database of adoptable pets—was functionally organizing data from hundreds of sources. Approximately 17,000 found/temporarily sheltered pets were listed and more than 22,000 rescue requests had been entered into the database.

Toonces, a 13-year-old, gray tabby cat with a predilection for bacon, was one of them.

Sarah Hoffman can trace her Louisiana roots back several generations. She was born in Metairie, Louisiana, just outside of New Orleans and grew up in a rural area, surrounded by pets. "At one point we had 20 cats," she says. "Of course, most of them lived outside. We had lots of animals, including a pig, and we had our own vegetable garden. It was like a small farm."

But of all the animals, Toonces was special.

"My mom adopted Toonces from a shelter

when I was about 13 years old," recalls Sarah. "We thought he looked just like a character on *Saturday Night Live:* Toonces the Driving Cat. So that's where he got his name.

"He was a very laid-back cat. He just wanted to lie around, hoping to be petted and maybe get some tuna once in a while. He was an indoor-outdoor cat, and he loved to sleep in the bed with me."

Until Hurricane Katrina tore through her neighborhood, Sarah lived in the Uptown area of New Orleans, one of the older areas of the city. "I live on Magazine Street, which is a very well known street in that part of New Orleans. There are a lot of little boutiques and antique shops and restaurants, so it gets a lot of tourists as well.

"I was at work and my boss, who's from Kansas, is pretty wary of any kind of storm. She's used to tornadoes, so any time there's a storm coming, she always evacuates. I don't always evacuate. I do occasionally, but I grew up here and am used to it."

In fact, Sarah wasn't planning to evacuate at all for Hurricane Katrina. She put off her boss's questions and concerns by saying she'd play it by ear the next day.

Saturday, August 27, 2005

On the Saturday before the hurricane, Sarah slept in and, upon waking, didn't feel very well. When her father called to tell her it would be a good idea to pack up and leave town, she balked. "I told him I wasn't feeling up to it. I was going to stay put."

She laughs as she recalls her father's insistence. "He finally convinced me, so I left with my dog and two cats. We all got together and caravanned to my aunt's house in Birmingham, Alabama."

Before heading to Birmingham, Sarah stopped at her mother's home. "She has two dogs, Toonces, plus a cockatiel named Lucy," says Sarah. "Mom was frantic. She had just gotten off work and she didn't feel like dealing with any of this either." After a quick discussion, they decided to just bring the dogs with them.

Toonces, explains Sarah, wasn't reliable about using a litter box, making it difficult to take him on long trips that ended at someone else's home. So they did what they had done in the past: They put out lots of food and water and a large storage container of cat litter on the kitchen floor. Then they locked Toonces and Lucy in to ride out the storm.

In Birmingham, Sarah and her family watched the hurricane cross over their home state. They were happy they had evacuated and relieved to see the damage didn't appear to be as bad as the 11th-hour forecasts had predicted for New Orleans. "Then the levees broke. We were all in shock. We didn't really know how bad it was going to be and what parts of the city were going to flood. On television, it looked like the whole area was going to be under 20 feet (6 m) of water.

"Then as we started getting more accurate reports as to how much flooding was in which areas, I was thinking about my Lucy and Toonces, especially about Toonces. I mean, I grew up with him. So I started trying to find out what kinds of organizations were able to get into the city. And at that time no one was being allowed to go in, except for FEMA (Federal Emergency Management Agency). The National Guard was keeping everybody else out."

A week after Katrina's assault on New Orleans, Sarah faced an indisputable fact: she would not be going home any time soon. So she moved to Lakemount, Georgia, to live with her sister.

On-line, Sarah found several organizations tracking pet victims of Katrina and she e-mailed them. Her worry escalated when she heard that New Orleans would be spraying the city extensively for mosquitoes. She realized that the mosquito spraying was essential after the intense storm and wet conditions of Katrina. However, she also knew that the spray would be dangerous to animals with compromised immune systems who might be wandering outside.

On the nola.com community chat site, Sarah posted a request to anyone who might be in her area to break in and feed Toonces. She knew that his food and water would be running low, as they hadn't expected to be away for so long. Unsure of how bad the flooding was at home, she hoped her dear childhood friend would be able to find high ground to ride out the flooding.

Weeks passed without word.

"I had been on Petfinder.com looking at posted photos of animals that had been rescued," says Sarah. "You look at hundreds of these pictures, and they start to look the same. A lot of the pictures are not well focused, and you think that it might be your pet, but you can't really tell."

Sarah spent night after night looking over the pictures posted on the Petfinder website, her hope gradually fading.

A few weeks after the storm, Sarah and her family traveled back home to check on the damage and to salvage whatever they could. Toonces and Lucy were nowhere to be found. The only evidence that they'd survived the flooding was paw prints along the muddy kitchen floor, leading out the back door where, apparently, someone had broken in to let the animals out.

On October 3, five weeks after the hurricane, Sarah came across a photograph on Petfinder. com that made her heart skip a beat. "It was a close-up of a cat making a kind of squinty-eyed looking face. I screamed, 'That's Toonces!' He had this laid-back, surfer cat look, a little squinty-eyed face like he's stoned or something."

Sarah e-mailed immediately, something she'd done a few times before regarding other cats who might possibly have been Toonces, without success. This time, however, she knew beyond a doubt that she had found Toonces.

The next morning there was an e-mail from the Vero Beach Humane Society, asking her if she needed to see more pictures to be sure it was Toonces.

She didn't.

She did have one question: "When can I

come and get him?"

Because Toonces was in rough shape, the Vero Beach Humane Society was reluctant to fly him out. "I was so excited. This whole ordeal has been so awful in so many ways, not just loss of life and loss of property, but also people are scattered everywhere. You don't have your normal support system that you're used to having with your friends. It's depressing. Then suddenly, this wonderful thing happens! I was just so thrilled I would have done anything to go and get Toonces," says Sarah.

Sarah drove for seven hours from Georgia to Vero Beach, Florida, to pick him up.

Once an overweight cat that begged bacon strips from friendly neighbors, Toonces was now emaciated and on fluids intravenously.

"He definitely recognized me," says Sarah. When she picked him up, she could feel his bones through his skin. She scratched under his chin and he perked up and started to purr.

From Toonces's records at Vero Beach,

Sarah knows he was picked up on September 19, where he was taken to an animal shelter in Baton Rouge and given medical care. Beyond that, Toonces's adventure remains a mystery to Sarah. How did he get to Vero Beach, 735 miles (1183 km) away? It will remain a mystery.

Toonces's partner in adventure—the family pet cockatiel, Lucy— was also rescued, although the Hoffmans don't know where she eventually went.

After his return home, Toonces was placed on a special diet as a result of kidney problems, but he's otherwise doing well.

Sarah is doing okay, too, she says. She now lives with her sister in Lakemount, Georgia. "I was able to enroll in school here. I had just started classes at the University of New Orleans when the hurricane hit. There is a small local, private college near where my sister lives that has let me register here. They waived all tuition and got me in classes."

Her major? Pre-veterinary medicine.

CHAPTER 8

The Good Samaritan

B orn and raised in New Orleans, Joseph Martin Bagnerise now lives in Calgary, Canada, with his wife, Rosemarie, and their son, Jullien. When the family heard about Katrina's path to New Orleans, their thoughts immediately veered to Joseph's father, Charles Bagnerise, and to Charles's two sisters, Ma Mina and Cille, all of whom lived in the Big Easy.

"We weren't really aware of the hurricane

> **QUOTE**
>
> "The first question which the priest and the Levite asked [on the Jericho Road] was: 'If I stop to help this man, what will happen to me?' But ... the good Samaritan reversed the question: 'If I do not stop to help this man, what will happen to him?'"
>
> *Martin Luther King, Jr.*

until that Sunday, August 28," recalls Rosemarie. "At a barbecue with our friends, someone mentioned the hurricane. That was the first I'd heard anything of it.

Charles didn't have a phone and, since most people had been evacuated by then, Joseph and Rosemarie knew they wouldn't be able to get in touch with anyone in New Orleans.

Glued to their television sets and hoping to spot Charles senior, the Bagnerises didn't get any information until Tuesday after the storm, when Charles Junior, Joseph's older brother, called from Chicago. He told Joseph that Ma Mina and Cille were okay, having evacuated before the storm hit. They were safe in Alabama with relatives. But Charles had heard nothing about their father.

"We had no way of getting in touch with Dad and didn't know what to do," says Rosemarie. "We were in constant communication with Chicago and watching the television to see if he'd show up. I thought we might just see him in the crowd."

But they didn't.

Joseph was certain his father was alive. "I know Dad's a trooper. He's survived two wives, a couple of world wars. But as it got longer and I didn't hear anything, I started to worry," Joseph's voice tapers off.

"There were all kinds of web sites where you could register missing people," says Rosemarie. "So we registered him on all of those. Every couple of hours I'd go to the Red Cross list to see if he'd shown up.

"On Thursday, September 6 at 4 o'clock in the afternoon, ten days after the hurricane, I typed his name into the Red Cross list ... and there he was."

Charles L. Bagnerise is a slight man of 82

years, with the same mischievous twinkle in his eye as his son. His slight frame belies the tightly coiled energy and enthusiasm that explode from him in conversation.

"New Orleanians usually don't get too worked up about hurricanes," Charles says. "The streets may be flooded, but the waters go down about two or three hours after the hurricane passes through. Then we get out of the house and start looking around."

But Hurricane Katrina would be different.

Sunday, August 28, 2005

"That Sunday, I went to church for 11 o'clock mass. As I walked from my house, I noticed that no buses passed by," remembers Charles. "When I went to Cabrini [the church], it was locked. I had an envelope I put in church every month, so I went to the rectory mailbox and I put the money in the mailbox."

On his way back home, a lady from Charles's neighborhood passed by and asked him where he was going. "I told her I was going home and she said that there's a big hurricane passing through."

Charles's neighbor dropped him off at a little donut and coffee shop on St. Bernard and Broad. It, too, was locked.

Charles went home to wait. The severe weather situation had caught Charles unprepared, but he faced it with calm fortitude. "That night—Sunday night—it started raining. All that rain. I took all the pictures off the wall—my pictures and my wife's pictures. I took them with me as I climbed the ladder into the attic and went to sleep."

He awoke Monday morning to the declining storm, and left the attic to check out the damage. "The water was rising in the house. When I climbed down, the water was up to here." He slashes his hand across his waist to indicate the level to which the water had risen. "I opened the door and there were helicopters all over the place. I started screaming, 'Help me somebody!

My name is Charles L. Bagnerise! I live at 4342 Van Avenue!' But they just passed and passed and passed."

So Charles retreated to the attic to wait. When he came back down a few hours later, the water had risen much higher and he noticed something else alarming: the house appeared to be sinking. "I went outside, and I started screaming again.

"Along came a good Samaritan, a guy by the name of Austin Herbert. He was in a boat and he said, 'Get in this boat.'" Charles pauses, and then leans forward to say emphatically, "'Get. In. This. Boat.'"

Spotting Austin's rescue boat, Charles's neighbors ventured out, and by the time the boat left the neighborhood, it was loaded down with Charles, Austin, and five others.

Austin Herbert took his boatload of Katrina survivors to his two-story house off St. Bernard.

"He had three other men up there; he was a God-saving man. He said he was going to get some food, so I gave him my last $20. I told him I have more money in the bank at home, but he said 'Don't worry about that, you can't go back to it. We'll survive'. So he went and got some food," says Charles.

"I stayed there, one, two, three, four days," Charles counts off the days on his fingers.

One of the elderly men had a bad leg and Charles used his background as an army medic to make him more comfortable. "Austin had all kinds of shampoo and lotions and I rubbed the man's leg down. He had a razor blade and I scraped all his legs to make them clean and comfortable. I even cut his toenails. He says his skin looks much better now."

Helicopters continued flying overhead, and the tiny group of survivors watched the activity from Austin's rooftop. A portable radio kept them in touch with what was happening in the city around them. "Austin got a mirror and he shined the mirror on that helicopter. The helicopter came down and picked up three ladies.

One lady had her briefcase, but the pilot said she couldn't take it on board. Her insurance policies and such were in it, so she give it to Austin and he put it away for her."

On that trip, the helicopter pilot took four women and two men—the most vulnerable of the group. The next day the helicopter returned to pick more people off the roof. Charles chose not to go with him.

"The helicopter pilot brought them to the Superdome, and at that time we heard the stadium was raising hell. Mayor Nagin made a speech, was crying because the police force quit on him," says Charles. "The governor didn't do anything. President Bush come out here; he didn't do a thing for him. Nagin says, 'My people are dying …'"

"Three days after, here come the military people with pistols and everything else," Charles postures aggressively, "'HEY YOU! GET OFF THAT ROOF,' they say. 'Come down and get in this boat.'"

He shrugs. "I got off the roof and jumped in the boat."

But Austin refused to go, choosing instead to stay with his property. "He says, 'I got to stay on my roof and mind my boat, because there's people will steal your boat.'"

Charles, along with a boat full of other residents, was taken to the Ernest N. Morial Convention Center. From there, helicopters took them to the Louis Armstrong New Orleans International Airport, where they boarded a plane for El Paso, Texas.

Two hours later, Charles arrived at the El Paso Civic Center with only the clothes on his back. "It dawned on me, I better call Joseph Martin. I asked a lady, could she find my son. She says, 'What's your son's name and where does he live?' I told her he lives in Calgary, Canada."

The Civic Center volunteer linked Charles and Joseph up on the phone. "When I heard Rosemarie and Joseph Martin were coming to get me, I thanked God. My son saved my life."

"We found him on Thursday and we arrived in El Paso Saturday morning," chimes in Rosemarie. "We had no idea what kind of shape he was in. Or whether he had suffered. But we knew he was alive and he was safe."

"When they came," interjects Charles. "I was a happy soul. Because if they hadn't, I don't know what I would have done. My son and his wife," Charles leans forward. "Saved. My. Life."

CHAPTER 9

The Blame Game

L ike most North Americans, businessman Wayne Rogaczewski watched the fallout of the biggest storm of the year in the comfort of a safe location far from the scene of destruction. In Wayne's case, it was his corporate apartment in St. Paul, Minnesota. However, because of his home in New Orleans, he had more personal interest in the outcome than most.

"When the levees broke, they started showing it on television," he says. "Our home is not far from an industrial canal, and the intracoastal waterway flows into there. When they mentioned that the West Bank was one of the levees that had been breached or compromised, I thought, 'That's it; there goes the house. We're done.' The thought of it knocked the air out of me."

But in the hours following the levee breaches, Wayne didn't see any pictures of devastation from his side of town. He began e-mailing people who might know, to ask about the damages in his neighborhood.

"On Thursday morning, there was an e-mail from someone on the same street who saw my post, saying that basically all our homes had varying degrees of wind damage, but no homes took in any water. He said we were spared," Wayne says with relief, having dodged the bullet. This time.

Experts have warned for years that New Orleans is on a collision path with disaster. Its proximity to the Gulf Coast makes every hurricane season a threat, a gamble played out to Mother Nature's whim. And while many in New Orleans escaped death and total devastation from Katrina, many more will return to lives completely ravaged by the after-effects of her wrath.

For Judy and Courtney Carter, who first returned home to the Ninth Ward on Thanksgiving weekend 2005, life has been irrevocably altered.

Charles Bagnerise now watches the rebuilding of New Orleans as it rolls out on the television screen in the safety and warmth of his son's home in Canada. Asked if he'll return, Charles shrugs.

It's a shrug that's seen around the country every time New Orleanians contemplate the future of their city. Will the city successfully rebuild? And what will it be like?

And, most chillingly, what will the next hurricane season be like? Have people learned anything in the aftermath of Hurricane Katrina that will mitigate the effects of the next extreme storm? For the citizens of New Orleans were affected, not just by the hurricane itself, but also by their own personal decisions to go or to stay, as well as decisions made by various levels of politicians.

In the space of a single week, Hurricane Katrina grew from a tropical depression to one of the most destructive hurricanes in U.S. history. She tore across four states, killing more than 1,000 citizens, then sputtered to a tropical depression 25 miles (200 km) south of Clarksville, Tennessee on August 30, 2005. Her rains and winds continued, steadily weakening, all the way north to Quebec, Canada.

As Katrina was downgraded, the world watched in horror while death tolls in Louisiana and Mississippi climbed. Then came news that two levees in New Orleans had been breached and water was flooding 80 percent of the city.

Along with the physical and environmental toll Katrina left in her wake, she also revealed some glaring problems with the human reaction to a disaster of this magnitude. Her winds had barely left the city before the blame game began. There was no shortage of recrimination and faultfinding finger-pointing, from the highest levels of the government right down to the citizens themselves. No one, it seemed, was immune to the scathing criticisms and blame that circulated immediately after the storm and for months afterwards. Accusations were made and refuted with breathtaking speed.

Some blamed the citizens themselves, for not evacuating when the storm's potential became known. Some blamed Mayor Nagin for not evacuating the city soon enough. Governor Blanco was criticized for her slow response. FEMA and its director, Michael Brown, came under fire for a delayed and sluggish post-hurricane rescue response. The harshest critics of the government—at the municipal, state, and federal levels—suggested that political posturing throughout the aftermath was merely for the benefit of photo opportunities.

Even the Red Cross was not immune from criticism as the world watched Louisiana struggle in a post-Katrina world.

Michael Marcavage, director of the Philadelphia-based evangelical organization known as Repent America, appeared to blame New Orleanians themselves—or perhaps God—when he said, "Although the loss of lives is deeply saddening, this act of God destroyed a wicked city. From 'Girls Gone Wild' to 'Southern Decadence,' New Orleans was a city that had its doors wide open to the public celebration of sin. From the devastation may a city full of righteousness emerge."

By Tuesday, August 30, the day after the hurricane, New Orleans found itself without power or drinking water. What it did have was looting, dwindling food stores, steadily rising waters, and fires. It was reported that 80 percent of the city was under water, as deep as 20 feet (6.1 m) in some places. Rescuers in helicopters and boats began plucking people off rooftops, but the help didn't come fast enough for many.

President Bush was one of the first to come under scathing criticism as he cut his vacation short—reportedly on August 30—a full day after Katrina's Louisiana landfall. He made his first visit to the area—an airplane flyover—on August 31.

Councilwoman Jackie Clarkson was quoted early on as saying the scarce, exhausted police force should have been used for performing search-and-rescue operations rather than controlling looting. An obviously distressed Mayor Nagin stated that he thought, "hundreds, most likely thousands" were dead in his city. At one point, he speculated the number could reach as high as 10,000.

To an angry and disbelieving public, Homeland Security Secretary Michael Chertoff announced, "We are extremely pleased with the response that every element of the federal government, all of our federal partners, have made to this terrible tragedy." Ironically, the much-criticized FEMA and its director,

Michael Brown, came under the purview of Homeland Security.

On September 1, the *Houston Chronicle* reported that 20-year-old Jabbar Gibson commandeered a yellow school bus to evacuate New Orleans, filling the bus with stragglers he picked up along the way and delivering them safely to the Houston Astrodome. When they were the first bus to arrive at the designated evacuation point, they were initially refused refuge. Gibson became something of a folk hero as bloggers around the country suggested that Jabbar Gibson replace Michael Brown as FEMA Director, since *he* had an evacuation plan for New Orleans.

As Jabbar Gibson evacuated his busload of people to Texas, looting, violence, and carjacking were reportedly increasing in New Orleans. In response, the military upped its National Guard deployment to 30,000.

Reports of looting and violence followed quickly on the heels of this storm, as they typically do after any devastating storm. One of the most dramatic post-hurricane stories centered on the reports of deaths and violence at the Morial Convention Center and the Superdome. Stories of Superdome rapes and of shots fired at potential rescuers filled the headlines and flashed across the nation's television screens. Some disputed the stories as sensationalist and untrue.

In the early days of the aftermath, gasoline prices spiked as high as $5 a gallon, as people rushed to the pumps in anticipation of a shortage. Oilrigs on the Gulf were found up to 17 miles (27 km) from their original locations.

On September 2, the U.S. Army Corps of Engineers announced that it would take up to 80 days to drain New Orleans, while President Bush acknowledged the criticisms of slow and inadequate response times. He admitted, "The results are not acceptable."

By Sunday, September 4—a week into the aftermath of Hurricane Katrina—the Superdome had been fully evacuated, with the evacuees bussed to secure locations outside of New Orleans. The U.S. Coast Guard had rescued 17,000 people and the New Orleans police department announced that two of its officers had committed suicide, victims of Katrina-related stress. Both men ended their lives with their own guns. More police officers had turned in their badges and some just didn't return to work.

Long after the storm, the bad news continued. Following the announcement that 250 police officers evacuated their posts without permission during Hurricane Katrina, Police Chief Eddie Compass resigned. On Thursday, September 29, the reputation of the New Orleans police department was further tarnished by accusations of a number of officers taking part in post-Katrina looting.

On Tuesday, October 4, Mayor Nagin announced that New Orleans would have to lay off half of its municipal workforce due to financial fallout from the hurricanes. It seemed the bad news would never end.

When the immediate crisis had passed and the casualties were totaled up and a surprising fact was reported. According to official statistics, only six people died in the Superdome after Hurricane Katrina, none of them violently. One overdosed, one was an apparent suicide, and four died of natural causes.

Unfolding the individual truths of Katrina's aftermath may take years to sort out. Some truths may never be fully known. Truth, it seems, is often in the heart of the teller.

CHAPTER 10

The Big Easy Bounces Back

On October 11, 2005, 43 days after Hurricane Katrina tore through the Big Easy, the U.S. Army Corps of Engineers declared New Orleans dry. On relatively high ground, the historic French Quarter emerged from Hurricane Katrina reasonably undamaged. Other areas of the city were not so fortunate.

Crews had worked round-the-clock to pump more than 224 billion gallons out of the city, beating out their worst-case estimate of 80 days by nearly half.

With the majority of the city underwater after the levee breach, there were fears that the contaminated standing water would promote the spread of hepatitis A, cholera, and typhoid fever. The toxic gumbo running through the streets of the city was a mix of gasoline, human waste, hospital waste, bleach, chemicals, and factory waste. But, according to Dr. John Pardue, director of the Louisiana Water Resources Institute at Louisiana State University, research suggests that the floodwater sludge was no more toxic than typical floodwater. Pardue was cautious, however, about the safety of a return to the city, citing concerns about mold growth and chemicals that had not rapidly evaporated.

Long-term environmental and health concerns after the flooding are still unclear. Certain areas are more clearly at risk because of their proximity to industrial plants, but the fears of toxic mold and carcinogenic dust stand as valid concerns. The answers may take months, or even years, as the Louisiana Department of Environmental Quality and the Environmental Protection Agency continue to test.

For evacuated residents, it's one more thing to worry about in their post-Katrina world.

The warm, moist conditions were favorable for mosquitoes, and the city mounted concentrated mosquito spraying in the hopes that mosquito-related diseases, such as malaria and West Nile virus, would be prevented.

As districts were examined and deemed safe, residents gradually returned. The last ward to open to residents was the Ninth Ward, home to Judy and Courtney Carter. Residents were allowed into the lower Ninth Ward beginning Wednesday, October 12, but only to view their homes and salvage what they could.

Around the city, daycare centers and schools remained closed, or opened with severely reduced numbers. New Orleans faced the last months of 2005 as a nearly childless city.

Many believed the children would not return as they settled with their families in far-flung towns and states across the country.

Mail service was restored to all areas of New Orleans by October 11, with over-the-counter service in any areas where postal carriers could not make deliveries.

Hotels and restaurants opened as soon as they were able, citing a lack of employees rather than a lack of customers as the reason for any delay. Their customers were aid workers, construction workers, journalists, and residents who needed a night out.

Louis Armstrong New Orleans International Airport opened for business on September 13 and Amtrak began rail service to and from New Orleans on October 9. On Sunday, October 2, the New Orleans Regional Transit Authority opened up four routes running limited hours seven days a week. Service was free for a firm six-month period.

Thursday, October 6 saw the opening of

the first major temporary trailer park for New Orleanians who had been left homeless by the storm. Nicknamed "FEMA Town" by some, it could potentially house more than 2,000 people. The trailers were arranged, town-like, with gravel streets and plans for postal service and bus connections. The trailers each provided between 200 and 300 square feet (18.6 and 27.9 m²) of living space, a welcome respite from the cramped evacuation quarters many had been living in.

THE IMPORTANCE OF MARDI GRAS

Total Mardi Gras Visitors:
6,135,890

Tourists Staying in Hotels:
985,890

Overall Spending:
$1,056,124,885

Source: The Official Tourism Site of the City of New Orleans (stats given for 2000)

Undeterred, Mardi Gras organizers announced on Wednesday, October 12, that they would go ahead with the annual event, scheduled for February 2006.

Dr. Moby Solangi of the beleaguered Gulfport Oceanarium

was also making plans. "We intend to rebuild bigger and better. What has happened has happened, and I think the coast is going to rebound. It's a small community and we've had organizations like SeaWorld and Gulfarium and Gulf World and the Navy helping us. Everybody we have talked to has offered us help, offered us places for the animals."

The story of the dolphins' survival served to uplift a state that had been brought to its knees by the killer storm, believes Moby. "The animals endured all of these hardships, too. If these animals can do that, so can we."

Posted on the Louis Armstrong New Orleans International Airport website after the hurricane:

Dear America,

I suppose we should introduce ourselves: We're South Louisiana.

We have arrived on your doorstep on short notice and we apologize for that, but we never were much for wait-ing around for invitations. We're not much on formalities like that.

And we might be staying around your town for a while, enrolling in your schools and looking for jobs, so we wanted to tell you a few things about us. We know you didn't ask for this and neither did we, so we're just going to have to make the best of it.

First of all, we thank you. For your money, your water, your food, your prayers, your boats and buses and the men and women of your National Guards, fire departments, hospitals and everyone else who has come to our rescue.

We're a fiercely proud and inde-pendent people, and we don't cotton much to outside interference, but we're not ashamed to accept help when we need it. And right now, we need it.

Just don't get carried away. For instance, once we get around to fishing again, don't try to tell us what kind of lures work best in your waters. We're not going to listen. We're stubborn that way.

You probably already know that we talk funny and listen to strange music and eat things you'd probably hire an exterminator to get out of your yard. We dance even if there's no radio. We drink at funerals. We talk too much and laugh too loud and live too large and, frankly, we're suspicious of those who don't. We put Tabasco on stuff without tasting it first.

But we'll try not to judge you while we're in your town.

Everybody loves their home, we know that. But we love South Louisiana with a ferocity that borders on the pathological. Sometimes we bury our dead in LSU sweatshirts.

Often we don't make sense. You may wonder why, for instance—if we could only carry one small bag of belongings with us on our journey to your state—why in God's name did we bring a pair of shrimp boots? We can't really explain that. It is what it is.

You've probably heard that many of us stayed behind. As bad as it is, many of us cannot fathom a life outside of our border, out in that place we call Elsewhere.

The only way you could understand that is if you have been there, and so many of you have. So you realize that when you strip away all the craziness and bars and parades and music and architecture and all that hooey, really, the best thing about where we come from is us.

We are what made this place a national treasure. We're good people.

And don't be afraid to ask us how to pronounce our names. It happens all the time.

When you meet us now and you look into our eyes, you will see the saddest story ever told. Our hearts are broken into a thousand pieces.

But don't pity us. We're going to make it. We're resilient. After all, we've been rooting for the Saints for 35 years. That's got to count for something.

OK, maybe something else you should know is that we make jokes at inappropriate times. But what the hell.

And one more thing: In our part of the country, we're used to having visitors. It's our way of life. So when all this is over and we move back home, we will repay to you the hospitality and generosity of spirit you offer to us in this season of our despair.

That is our promise. That is our faith.

Thank you,
South Louisiana

A Timeline of Hurricane Katrina

Tuesday, August 23, 2005
>The U.S. National Hurricane Center releases a statement advising that Tropical Depression Twelve is forming over the southeastern Bahamas, about 350 miles (563 km) east of Miami.

Wednesday, August 24, 2005
>At 11 a.m., Tropical Depression Twelve, now strengthened and more organized, is named Tropical Storm Katrina, becoming the 11th named storm of 2005.

Thursday, August 25, 2005
>The National Hurricane Center declares Katrina a Category 1 hurricane, and she lumbers ashore in south Florida

between Hallandale Beach and North Miami Beach. Governor Jeb Bush declares a state of emergency in Florida. Ultimately, 11 people die in Florida as a result of Hurricane Katrina's assault.

Friday, August 26, 2005

Katrina weakens briefly to a tropical storm, and then moves out to the Gulf of Mexico, where she grows to a Category 2 hurricane, veering north and west toward Mississippi and Louisiana. Governor Blanco declares a state of emergency in Louisiana.

Saturday, August 27, 2005

Katrina is upgraded to a Category 3 hurricane and barrels towards Louisiana. The National Hurricane Center warns Morgan City, Louisiana, to the Alabama-Florida border that the hurricane is expected in that area within the next 24 hours. Mayor Nagin declares

a state of emergency and issues a voluntary evacuation order. President Bush declares a state of emergency in Louisiana and highways leading out of New Orleans are clogged with evacuating traffic. Several major interstates convert to one-way routes out of New Orleans.

Sunday, August 28, 2005

At 2 a.m., Katrina is a Category 4 hurricane. She is escalated to a Category 5 hurricane five hours later. At 10 a.m., Mayor Nagin issues a mandatory evacuation order—the first in New Orleans history—and opens 10 "refuges of last resort," including the Superdome. The National Guard and the police work on evacuating those left behind, conducting security and screening at the Superdome. Bob Riley, Governor of Alabama, issues a state of emergency, and evacuation orders are declared all along the Mississippi coast.

Monday, August 29, 2005

At 4 a.m., Hurricane Katrina is downgraded to a Category 4. She makes first landfall near Buras, Louisiana, at 6:10 a.m. As Katrina rips through New Orleans, a section of the Superdome tears off, two major flood-control levees are breached, and the National Weather Service reports total structural failure in areas of New Orleans. Many are believed dead. Governor Haley Barbour of Mississippi says dozens are feared dead in his state. Twelve hours after making landfall, Hurricane Katrina is downgraded to a tropical storm.

Tuesday, August 30, 2005

Left without power and drinking water, New Orleans faces rising waters from major levee breaches and looting and fires in parts of the city. Governor Blanco says the Superdome must be evacuated, and

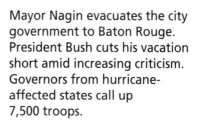

Mayor Nagin evacuates the city government to Baton Rouge. President Bush cuts his vacation short amid increasing criticism. Governors from hurricane-affected states call up 7,500 troops.

Wednesday, August 31, 2005

Governor Blanco ratchets up the pressure to evacuate the Superdome, while additional National Guard forces pour into the area. Mayor Nagin calls for a total evacuation as President Bush flies over the affected area on his way to Washington. Nagin speculates that thousands of people are likely dead in Katrina's wake.

Thursday, September 1, 2005

Criticism of FEMA and all levels of government continue to escalate as Governor Blanco calls for 40,000 troops. President George W. Bush pushes Congress for $10.5 billion in aid and appoints his father—

former President George H.
W. Bush—and former Presi-
dent Bill Clinton to mount a
fundraising effort. As rescuers attempt to save trapped
residents, reports of violence
surge. Gasoline prices spike
and shortages are reported in
some areas.

Friday, September 2, 2005

President Bush meets with
Governor Blanco and Mayor
Nagin, and visits the 17th Canal
breach. The Convention Center
is now secure and the National
Guard is bringing in convoys of
food and water.

Friday, September 9, 2005

Homeland Security Secretary,
Michael Chertoff, announces
Coast Guard Vice Admiral Thad
Allen to replace much-criticized
Michael Brown as the site head
of relief operations in the
Gulf Coast.

Monday, September 12, 2005
> Michael Brown resigns from FEMA. He is replaced the following day by Miami native David Paulison.

Tuesday, September 27, 2005
> Police Chief Eddie Compass resigns without explanation, following the announcement that 250 police officers evacuated their posts without permission during Hurricane Katrina.

Tuesday, October 4, 2005
> Mayor Nagin announces that 3,000 city employees will be laid off for economic reasons related to Hurricane Katrina and Rita.

Friday, October 28, 2005
> Forty-five police officers and six civilian employees are fired for abandoning their posts during Hurricane Katrina.

Late Fall 2005—Update

- Hundreds of bodies remain unclaimed; Louisiana coroners are unable to identify bodies of hundreds more—FEMA and Louisiana state officials disagree on who should pay for DNA testing.
- The Army Corps of Engineers expresses concern that engineers may not have time to completely rebuild levees before the 2006 hurricane season.
- First Katrina-related lawsuits surface.

Amazing Facts and Figures

HURRICANE PAM EXERCISE

On July 23, 2004, Hurricane Pam, a disaster-planning exercise designed to predict the outcome of a Category 3 hurricane in Louisiana, is concluded. Its findings: A Category 3 hurricane would cause up to 20 inches (508 mm) of rain in parts of southeast Louisiana and storm surge that topped levees in the New Orleans area.

The disaster plan exercise brought together officials from 50 parish, state, federal, and volunteer organizations for a five-day examination of what would happen under sustained winds of 120 miles (193 km) per hour, 20 inches (508 mm) of rain, and a storm surge topping levees in New Orleans. According to the exercise, Hurricane Pam destroyed 600,000 buildings and forced the evacuation of more than a million residents.

THE DIFFERENCE BETWEEN A WATCH AND A WARNING

A hurricane watch advisory means that hurricane conditions are possible within the next 36 hours. A warning means hurricane conditions are expected within the next 24 hours.

HOW TO PREPARE FOR A HURRICANE WATCH

1 Track the hurricane progress on a battery-operated radio

2 Top up your car's gas tank

3 Check your emergency supplies

4 Move outdoor items into a garage or shed; anchor any items that can't be stored

5 Close and board up windows

6 Remove outside antennas

7 Turn your refrigerator and freezer to their coldest settings and avoid opening them

8 Fill tubs, jugs, and bottles with drinking water

9 Store valuables in waterproof containers in the highest parts of the house

10 Review your evacuation plan

Deadliest Storms

Rank	Hurricane	Year	Category	Deaths*
1	Galveston, Texas	1900	4	8,000+
2	Florida	1928	4	2,500+
3	Louisiana	1893	4	1,100+
4	South Carolina & Georgia	1893	3	1,000+
5	South Carolina & Georgia	1881	2	700
6	Florida Keys	1935	5	408
7	Louisiana	1856	4	400
8	Texas & Louisiana (Audrey)	1957	4	390
9	Florida, Alabama & Mississippi	1926	4	372
10	Louisiana	1909	3	350

Does not include offshore deaths
Source: National Hurricane Center

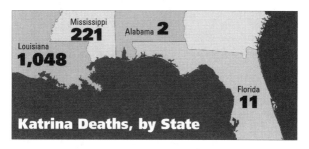

Mississippi **221** Alabama **2**

Louisiana **1,048**

Florida **11**

Katrina Deaths, by State

The Saffir-Simpson Scale

The Saffir-Simpson Scale measures hurricanes on a scale from 1 to 5, based on the hurricane's intensity.

	Winds	Damage Potential
Category 1	74–95 mph (119–153 kph)	• some damage to mobile homes and signs; • coastal flooding;
Category 2	96–110 mph (154–177 kph)	• some damage to roofs, doors, and windows; • flooding damages piers; • small craft may break their moorings; • some trees blown down;
Category 3	111–130 mph (178–209 kph)	• some structural damage to small residences and utility buildings; • large trees blown down; • mobile homes and poorly built signs destroyed; • flooding near the coast destroys smaller structures with larger structures damaged by floating debris; • terrain may be flooded well inland;

	Winds	Damage Potential
Category 4	131–155 mph (210–249 kph)	• more extensive failure of non-bearing exterior walls with some complete roof structure failure on small residences; • major erosion of beach areas; • terrain may be flooded well inland;
Category 5	156 mph (250 kph) and up	• complete roof failure on many residences and industrial buildings; • some complete building failures with small utility buildings blown over or away; • flooding damages lower floors of all structures near the shoreline; • massive evacuation of residential areas may be required.

WORLDWIDE SUPPORT FOR KATRINA VICTIMS

The devastation caused by Katrina sparked a world-wide outpouring of help, including support from the following countries:

- Australia announced a $10 million donation to the Red Cross, slated for victims of Hurricane Katrina. A team of emergency management specialists was also dispatched to the U.S. to help with recovery.
- Austria offered up to 10 disaster relief experts, four water purification units, high capacity pumps, and security personnel.
- Canada deployed more than 1,000 Canadian Forces personnel, three Canadian Forces ships, one Canadian Coast Guard vessel, three Sea King helicopters, 35 Navy divers, as well as healthcare and equipment support.
- China offered $5 million and rescue workers.
- France offered a civil defense detachment of 35 people, tents, camp beds, generators, motor pumps, water treatment units, emergency kits, 2 CASA aircraft capable of airlifting 4.4 tons of supplies, a ship, a frigate (*Ventose*) with its Panther helicopter, and a hurricane disaster unit of 20 soldiers with 1984 pounds (900 kg) of specialized supplies and medical support.

WORLDWIDE SUPPORT FOR KATRINA VICTIMS

- Great Britain offered 500,000 standard issue ration packs, medical teams, water purification units, camp beds, blankets, and specialist personnel.
- Norway offered $1.6 million (through the United Nations and the Red Cross), emergency personnel, five military divers, medicine, and equipment.
- Singapore offered three Chinook helicopters and 38 RSAF personnel.
- Sri Lanka (itself recovering from the destruction and 30,000 fatalities of the 2004 tsunami) donated $25,000 to the American Red Cross, on behalf of its people.

HOW TO HELP

American Red Cross: 800-435-7669
AmeriCares: 800-486-HELP
Farm Aid Inc: 800-FARM-AID
Habitat for Humanity: 229-924-6935
The Humane Society of the U.S.: 302-258-8276
Salvation Army: 800-725-2769
United Way of America: 800-272-4630
Log on to www.rc-katrina.com

Flooded Areas of New Orleans

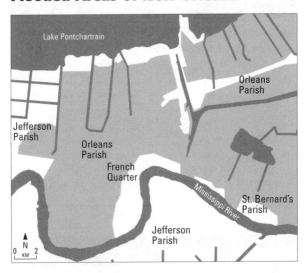

New Orleans Cross Section

Source: The Washington Post

New Orleans Racial Makeup

	New Orleans	US Average
Percentage Black	66.7%	18.5%
Black per capita annual income	$11,332	$14,025
White per capita annual income	$31,971	$36,700
Black poverty rate	35%	27.5%
White poverty rate	11.5%	12.2%

The lowest areas of the city are the hardest hit, with 80 percent of New Orleans under water.

Flood Wall

Gentilly Ridge U of New Orleans

Lake Pontchartrain
(usual level)

Costliest Storms*

Rank	Hurricane	Year	Category	Damage**
1	Andrew (FL, LA)	1992	5	$43.7B
2	Charley (FL)	2004	4	$15.0B
3	Ivan (FL, AL)	2004	3	$14.2B
4	Hugo (SC)	1989	4	$12.3B
5	Agnes (FL, NE US)	1972	1	$11.3B
6	Betsy (FL, LA)	1965	3	$10.8B
7	Frances (FL)	2004	2	$8.9B
8	Camille (MS, LA, VA)	1969	5	$8.9B
9	Diane (NE US)	1955	1	$7.0B
10	Jeanne (FL)	2004	3	$6.9B

* More than half the population of the United States (150 million people) resides in coastal areas which are at risk of hurricanes, flooding, and other weather calamities. More than 23 million Americans live in areas where a hurricane catastophe is inevitable at some time in the future.

** In billions. 2004 dollars adjusted for inflation.

As of October 17, 2005. Damage by Hurricane Rita, close on the heels of Katrina, is also reflected in these numbers.
Source: FEMA, Release Date: October 17, 2005 (Release Number: 1603-089)

1.3 MILLION LOUISIANANS APPLIED FOR STATE & FEDERAL DISASTER ASSISTANCE

FEMA approved in excess of $3.3 Billion for emergency assistance and disaster housing

13,609 evacuees remained in 169 shelters in the state

Families and relief workers occupied **2,400** travel trailers

An additional

6,901

housing units (including travel trailers, extended-stay apartments, hotels, and cruise ships) are in use

7.4 million cubic yards (5.6 million m³) of garbage was removed

IN EXCE$$ OF $46.5 MILLION IN LOAN$ WA$ APPROVED BY THE U.$. $MALL BUSINE$$ ADMINI$TRATION FOR U$E BY PEOPLE AND BU$INE$$ES AFFECTED BY THE HURRICANE($)

The American Red Cross served more than 3.8 million meals and provided shelter for 141,018 people

- 1,691 TRUCKLOADS OF WATER
- 1,485 TRUCKLOADS OF ICE
- 1,195 TRUCKLOADS OF TARPS
- 1,011 TRUCKLOADS OF MREs (MEALS READY TO EAT) WENT TO AFFECTED AREAS

The Salvation Army served more than 1.1 million meals

296,953 INSPECTIONS WERE COMPLETED ON DAMAGED HOMES

35,800 TEMPORARY ROOFS WERE INSTALLED AS PART OF THE U.S. ARMY CORPS OF ENGINEERS' OPERATION BLUE ROOF

34 Disaster Recovery Centres assisted more than **20,751** residents

What People Said

"Hurricane planning in Louisiana will continue. Over the next 60 days, we will polish the action plans developed during the Hurricane Pam exercise. We have also determined where to focus our efforts in the future."

Michael Brown, Deputy Director for Emergency Preparedness of Disaster Plan Exercise, Hurricane Pam

"Some levees in the area could be overtopped."

National Weather Service and the National Hurricane Center (NHC Storm Advisory 26, August 29, 2005)

"That Category 4 hurricane caused the same kind of damage that we anticipated. So we planned for it two years ago. Last year, we exercised it. And unfortunately this year, we're implementing it."

Michael Brown, FEMA Director,
referring to 2004 Disaster
Plan Exercise, Hurricane Pam

"I don't think anybody anticipated the breach of the levees."

President Bush on "Good Morning
America," September 1, 2005

"Don't Try. I am sleeping inside with a big dog, an ugly woman, two shotguns, and a claw hammer."

Sign Outside Bob Rue's
New Orleans Oriental Rug Store

"Brownie, you're doing a heck of a job."

President Bush to now former
FEMA director Michael Brown,
Mobile Regional Airport Mobile, Alabama

"Considering the dire circumstances
that we have in New Orleans—virtually
a city that has been destroyed—
things are going relatively well."

Michael Brown,
FEMA Director on CNN,
September 3, 2005

"This looks like the hull of a slave ship."

Reverend Jesse Jackson, on visiting the New Orleans Convention Center where thousands of people were stranded

"No one would ever believe that this is a day in the life of America."

Courtney Carter, New Orleans evacuee

"One of the true tests of leadership is the ability to recognize a problem before it becomes an emergency."

Arnold Glasow, author

"What I'm hearing, which is sort of scary, is they all want to stay in Texas. Everyone is so overwhelmed by the hospitality. And so many of the people in the arena here, you know, were underprivileged anyway, so this—this is working very well for them."

Barbara Bush, First Mom,
in the Houston Astrodome

"Excuse me, Senator, I'm sorry for interrupting. I haven't heard that, because, for the last four days, I've been seeing dead bodies in the streets here in Mississippi. And to listen to politicians thanking each other and complimenting each other, you know, I got to tell you, there are a lot of people here who are very upset, and very angry, and very frustrated."

Anderson Cooper, CNN journalist,
speaking to Senator Mary Landrieu
on CNN, September 1, 2005

"Bureaucracy has murdered people in the greater New Orleans area. And bureaucracy needs to stand trial before Congress today. ... So, I'm asking Congress, please investigate this now. Take whatever idiot they have at the top of whatever agency and give me a better idiot. Give me a caring idiot. Give me a sensitive idiot. Just don't give me the same idiot."

Aaron Broussard, president of Jefferson Parish, on CBS's Early Show, September 6, 2005

"My biggest mistake was not recognizing by Saturday that Louisiana was dysfunctional."

Michael Brown, now former Director of FEMA to a congressional panel set up by House Republican leaders to investigate the hurricane response

Glossary

Eye: the center of the storm, where it is relatively calm. Winds in the round or elliptical eye are 15 mph (24 kph) or less and the air is hot and humid.

Eyewall: the area of highest winds and greatest violence, surrounding the eye.

Hurricane: a tropical cyclone with winds exceeding 74 mph (119 kph). The word "hurricane" typically refers to storms in the Atlantic Basin.

Hurricane Season: that part of the year most likely to produce hurricanes. In the Atlantic, Caribbean, and Gulf of Mexico, the season runs from June 1 to November 30.

Landfall: the junction of the surface center of a hurricane with the coastline. It is not necessarily the point of the strongest winds.

Millibar: a measure of air pressure used by the National Weather Service. The lower the millibars, the lower the pressure and, generally, the more intense the storm.

Saffir-Simpson Hurricane Scale: ranks storms

according to wind speed and their subsequent potential for damage.

Storm Surge: the large wall of water—between 50 to 100 miles (84 to 161 km) wide—that crashes onto land when the hurricane makes landfall.

Tornadoes: form in the outer bands of the hurricane, as well as closer to the eyewall.

Tropical Cyclone: a term to broadly describe cyclonic storms originating over tropical and subtropical ocean waters.

Tropical Disturbance: a dense cluster of tropical thunderstorms over a sustained period of 24 hours. Tropical disturbances are not unusual over the North Atlantic and only a small number of these will develop into hurricanes.

Tropical Depression: conditions that could develop into a hurricane. Winds are less than 39 mph (63 kph). The circular motion associated with hurricane formation can be seen, but typically located only near the ocean surface.

Tropical Storm: stronger than a tropical depression. A tropical storm presents with sustained winds of between 39 and 73 mph (63–117 kph) with signs of becoming better organized and more intense. It is capable of doing considerable wind and flood damage.

Typhoon: a hurricane in the western Pacific Ocean.

Select Bibliography

Allaby, Michael. *How Weather Works.* London: Dorling Kindersley Limited, 1995.

Allaby, Michael. *Hurricanes* Facts on File, Inc., 1995.

Huler, Scott. *de-fin-ing the wind.* New York: Crown Publishers, 2004.

Web sites
Federal Emergency Management Agency. Hurricane Katrina Recovery Information: www.fema.gov/press/2005/resources_katrina.shtm

National Aeronautics and Space Administration. Hurricane Resource Page: www.nasa.gov/vision/earth/lookingatearth/hurricane_2005.html

National Oceanic & Atmospheric Administration. *A Bird's Eye View of Hurricane Katrina's Destruction.* www.noaanews.noaa.gov/stories2005/s2539.htm

National Hurricane Center: www.nhc.noaa.gov/

State of Louisiana, Governor Kathleen Babineaux Blanco: www.gov.state.la.us/

The Hurricane Watch Net: www.hwn.org/home/atlantic.html

The White House. Hurricane Relief: www.whitehouse.gov/infocus/hurricane/

Weather.com. Hurricane Central: www.weather.com/newscenter/tropical/

Acknowledgements

A big thank you to my husband and my dearest friend, Ted, who has weathered all of life's storms with me. Thanks also to my children, Brandon and Courtney, who have never stopped listening to my stories.

Thank you to the good people who shared their stories with me in this book. To a person, they spoke with unflinching honesty. They represent the true heroes of the storm, and the heart and soul of New Orleans.

To my critique group of Diana Scott, Carol Mulholland, and Leanne Baugh-Peterson, thank you for your writing wisdom and your friendship. I can think of no finer folk to rage against the ages with.

Finally, thank you to Altitude Publishing for the opportunity to tell Katrina's amazing stories. To publisher Stephen Hutchings, associate publisher Kara Turner and to my editor, Frances

Purslow, I very much appreciate your encouragement, support, and gentle direction. Thank you again for this opportunity to tell the stories of Katrina.

Photo Credits

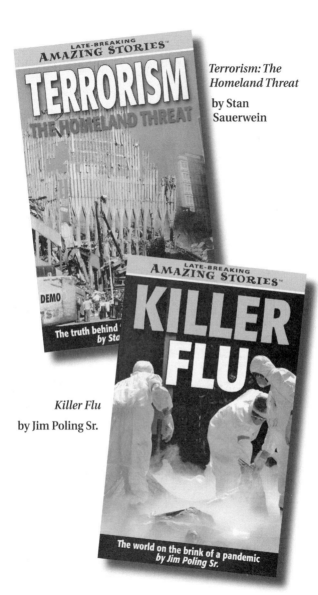

Terrorism: The Homeland Threat

by Stan Sauerwein

Killer Flu

by Jim Poling Sr.

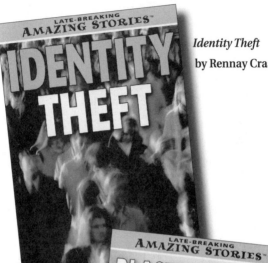

Identity Theft
by Rennay Craats

Plastic Surgery Gone Wrong

by Melanie Jones

CSI: The truth behind crime scene investigation

by Jane I. Fielding

Crystal Meth

by Nate Hendley

Wrongfully Accused

by Nora Rock

China: the Next Monster Power?

by Nate Hendley

Hurricane Hell
by Dee van Dyk

Water Matters
by Moushumi
Chakrabarty

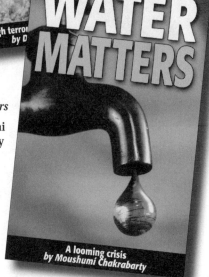